DATE DUE

261-2500

Printed
in USA

Guide To LOCAL AREA NETWORKS

TJ BYERS

A SPECTRUM BOOK

Micro Text Publications, Inc.
Prentice-Hall, Inc., Englewood Cliffs, New Jersey 07632

DEDICATION

Dedicated to a fighting Marine who survived the hells of Beirut, Lebanon, October, 1983--our son, Joseph.

ACKNOWLEDGEMENTS

I wish to express my sincere appreciation to Joseph Bernard, M'Lou Ishmiel, Jane Nichols, Ed Powers, and Beverly Toms for their help in assembling this book. Illustrations are by Forsfull Communications, William Giallo, and Garth Phillipsen.

Library of Congress Cataloging in Publication Data

Byers,TJ
    Guide to local area networks

    "A Spectrum Book."
    Includes index.
    1.   Local area networks (Computer networks)
I.   Title.
TK5105.7.B94   1984   001.64'404   84-18156
ISBN 0-13-369679-0
ISBN 0-13-369661-8 (pbk.)

10 9 8 7 6 5 4 3 2 1

ISBN 0-13-369679-0

ISBN 0-13-369661-8 {PBK.}

This book is available at a special discount when ordered in bulk quantities. Contact Prentice-Hall, Inc., General Publishing Division, Special Sales, Englewood Cliffs, N.J. 07632.

Prentice-Hall International, Inc., *London*
Prentice-Hall of Australia Pty. Limited, *Sydney*
Prentice-Hall Canada, Inc., *Toronto*
Prentice-Hall of India Private Limited, *New Delhi*
Prentice-Hall of Japan, Inc.,*Tokyo*
Prentice-Hall of Southeast Asia Pte. Ltd., *Signapore*
Whitehall Books Limited, *Wellington, New Zeland*
Editora Prentice-Hall do Brasil Ltda., *Rio de Janeiro*

CONTENTS

PREFACE

Local area networks are an innovation in computer technology which gives computers the ability to communicate among themselves. Their introduction has completely revolutionized our concept of the computer as a whole. In fact, networking is the fastest growing field in the computer industry.

That's why it should come as no surprise that precious little practical information exists. Consequently, until now the potential network buyer has had to make decisions based largely on myth and misinformation. The purpose of this book is to unravel the mysteries surrounding local area networks and give the reader a clear view of the technology.

This book is written specifically with the business professional in mind. It is well illustrated, with every caption containing a summary of the subject at hand, so that the captions alone give the general concepts of networking in just a few minutes. In-depth analysis of the material is provided in the easy-to-read text.

No prior knowledge of computers or networks is necessary; all the basics are reviewed. You begin with the basics of networking: what they are, why they exist, and how they can benefit you directly. Much preparation has been given to the first three chapters. These chapters answer the question "Is a local area network right for you?" After reading these chapters, you will know.

From here the book takes you in hand and walks you through the world of networking. Included in the analysis are alternative choices, protocol standards, and even a section on computer/network security—a hot topic in these times. Attention is paid throughout to network performance versus cost effectiveness.

The technical information presented in this book is not meant to make you a LAN design engineer. It is intended, instead, to familiarize you with the options and jargon you are likely to encounter in your quest for the perfect network. It is designed to give you the background you need to intelligently plan and discuss networking.

After the tutorial, you are exposed to real-world networks. Chapter 14 includes a listing of all the local area networks on the market today, their features, prices, and application areas. The recently released IBM PC Network for the AT computer is discussed in Chapter 15.

By the time you close the back cover, you will have a thorough understanding of networks and be in a position to talk confidently about the subject and make the networking decision that is right for you and your application.

WHAT IS A LOCAL AREA NETWORK?

Since the turn of the century, technology has been shaping our lives and lifestyles at an ever-increasing pace. Though we are often reluctant at first to accept a new technology as anything other than innovation, we gradually grow to accept the conveniences offered.

Once in a while, however, the technology works its magic on us in mysterious ways—ways never anticipated. The invention of the automobile, for instance, didn't spark a mechanical revolution, as some folks would like to believe. No, indeed, it launched us into an era of mass transportation. With its development came individual freedom of movement unsurpassed in history.

In a similar fashion, the computer has quietly ushered in a communications revolution. Instead of being the monstrous number-crunching calculator so many of us envisioned a few years ago, the computer has become the vehicle of mass communications.

It is communications which has raised us above the other animals. Through our ability to exchange thoughts and ideas, we have evolved into the society we are today. It can be said that the compulsion to strive for better and faster communications is more of an inbred need than a passing desire.

Out of this need to communicate have evolved communications networks—all sorts of networks. Over the ages we have assembled networks out of everything from drums to smoke signals to pony expresses get our message across. Computers are only our most recent tool in this quest. Unquestionably, communications networks are a part of our very existence.

This book deals with the newest of these networks, the local area network. Of course, new concepts must be digested a step at a time, and I plan to go step by step in this book. A good place to begin is by defining a communications network in general.

COMMUNICATIONS NETWORKS

Communications networks come in every size and shape imaginable, from the very small to the very large. In fact, networks are defined by their size. Since ancient times we have pushed to expand the boundaries of our communications area. The usefulness of a network, however, has always been limited by the speed at which the information can be sent—which has also been a limiting factor in network size.

The breakthrough came with the discovery of electronic communications, sparked by the invention of the telegraph, and followed by the telephone. At last, communications could be made at the speed of light over a wide area. Networks grew in size as a result.

Today's telecommunications networks allow us to talk around the world as easily as next door, and they are perfect examples of what are defined as *wide area networks*. They cover a wide area effectively.

Before the advent of wide area networks, business communications were limited. It could take weeks to get a response to a query. Wide area networks have changed business forever.

LOCAL AREA NETWORKS

It is generally accepted fact, however, that more than three-fourths of all business correspondence occurs at the local level. Although long-distance communications are essential, it is often more important to get a message across a room, than it is to talk across a continent.

WHAT IS A LOCAL AREA NETWORK?

This urgency also applies to computers. But until recently, the local aspect of everyday computer communications has been largely ignored. There has always been an unquestionable need for computers to talk among themselves at a distance, but the local problem was seldom considered. The eventual recognition of local needs gave birth to the *local area network*, or LAN for short.

A local area network is distinguished from other networks by the area it serves. Essentially, the local area network was devised to handle the needs of a local community. But actually defining the size of a local area network is tricky at best. In its most general sense, it is probably no larger than five miles across. However, this is very open to interpretation. If you conduct your business within the confines of a single office, then your office area dictates your network size. If on the other hand, you occupy a building or several buildings, you draw your boundaries accordingly. In other words, you set the limits of your local area network according to your workspace. As a rule of thumb, though, most network vendors limit the local area network performance to a few thousand feet.

On the other end, the only thing smaller than a local area network is the bus network contained inside your computer. It measures only inches across. It can be said that in size and appearance the local area network falls somewhere between the normal telecommunications networks and the bus networks used to interconnect computer devices within a cabinet. The technology used to develop LANs has been borrowed from both, with an amazing result that mimics neither.

LAN ADVANTAGES

Another distinguishing feature of local area networks is that they do not use public services or utilities. The network stands on its own, and it is yours to do with as you please. As long as you keep to yourself and disturb no one else, no restrictions or regulations apply to its use.

Although digital data transmission is currently the single most important use of a local area network, there is no reason to limit its capability. Voice, text, and even video transmissions are all possible through a properly designed network. In fact, upward compatibility and expansion are two of the strongest features of a LAN.

Local area networks have, for good reason, captured the imagination of many individuals. They offer an ideal solution to an unanswered problem. They are cheap, easy to install, omnipresent, and expandable. For this reason, more than any other, interest in local area networks has suddenly blossomed. Local area networks have matured almost overnight from a curiosity into an absolute necessity.

The need to communicate goes to the very core of our exsistence. In fact, the ability to communicate is what has raised us above other animals, and we constantly strive for faster and better communications. The computer is but another tool in this quest. Local area networks provide the communication link necessary for computers to talk among themselves.

2

WHY DO I NEED A LAN?

Why do you need a local area network? To communicate, of course! Communications form the backbone of modern business, and computer communications are no exception.

"Okay," you say, "I'm convinced communications are important in today's business world. But just where does a local area network fit into my scheme of things?"

I'm glad you asked. Local area networks belong any place you have a computer, computer terminal, or the need for processing power. In this information age, that is everywhere. LANs belong in the office, in the factory, and in the field. Still skeptical? Let's see how your present office could benefit from a local area network.

LAN IN THE OFFICE

Most small-business, professional, general-management, and executive offices still live in the dark ages. Most experts refer to it as the preindustrial era. In a preindustrial office, little conscious attention is paid to such things as systematic data flow, the efficiency or productivity of work methods, or modern information handling techniques. Emphasis is often placed, instead, on the volume production of the individual worker.

The few information devices that are present usually amount to telephones, copiers, and maybe even a word processor. Although these devices may be instrumental in office operation, no deliberate effort has been made to get maximum performance from them. Whether you realize it or not, the preindustrial office is unequipped for handling either a large volume of transactions or complex procedures requiring coordination of a variety of data sources. In fact, one of the most prolific (yet cost-consuming) activities around such an office is the making of multiple copies, filing the copies in various cabinets, and retrieving them. As a whole, the system is out of date and inefficient.

Fortunately, streamlining the preindustrial office to bring it up to information-age standards is not all that difficult. Believe it or not, you probably already have everything you need in your office right now. If you have a word processor, an advanced copier or

Local area networks make it possible for computers to communicate among themselves. Computer communications have many faces and can support varied needs. For example, LANs allow valuable resources, such as printers and data bases, to be shared, thereby reducing costs and maximizing equipment utilization. The economics of interfacing the modern office with a local area network can bring down the cost of producing a letter from $7 to $2. It is estimated by the year 1990 that some 38 million computerized workstations of various kinds are likely to be installed in offices, factories, and schools. The future success of business will lie in the ability of these workstations to communicate.

printer, and a personal computer or two, you can get started right now. All you need to do is connect all those lone devices together so they can talk to each other. This is where a local area network comes in.

RESOURCE SHARING

Let's take that printer, for example. It's a nice, letter-quality/ graphics printer that I know set you back a bundle, and understandably you can afford only one. But are you using it to its full advantage? Check out the line of people waiting to use it. You've probably seen shorter lines at Disneyland. And during lunches and breaks, that same printer sits idle.

With a simple connection to a local area network through a buffer, you could turn that printer into a really productive piece of equipment. Instead of waiting in line to access the printer, your people can simply request its use through the network. If the printer happens to be busy at the time, the buffer will store the data in memory and print it out after the printer has finished its prior assignments. In the meantime, your worker can go back to something besides discussing Johnny Carson or how badly the home team is doing.

What you are doing, in essence, is sharing a resource within your office. In this case, it happens to be a printer. You can also share human resources with a LAN. Let's say your secretary has a report due by the end of the week, but the work is just too much for one person. In the old days, you would have divided the job into halves, assigning each half to an employee, and pasting everything together at the end of the week, hoping the halves would fit reasonably well.

Sharing word processing or personal computer power, two workers could write the document at the same time, comparing notes along the way through network communications, to produce a smooth-flowing, intelligible report. No hasty rewrites, no duplication of effort, just one job well done.

Resource sharing also extends to mainframe computers, mass data storage, file servers—and telephones. Wherever a centralized need exists, the LAN can serve it efficiently.

ECONOMICS

Economics is another major factor in using a local area network. It is becoming far cheaper to communicate electronically than to communicate on paper. The transition to word processing with LAN interfacing can reduce secretarial costs from $7 per letter to less than $2. The savings are even more dramatic when you use electronic mail. The current cost of sending a letter via electronic mail is down to 30 cents or less.

Electronic filing, in which documents are stored and indexed in a computer memory, brings further savings. Through the use of a local area network, these files become available to everyone at the touch of a finger. Just imagine how much time can be saved between sales, accounting, and shipping, alone, with the use of a master computer file. No more invoices in triplicate, no more lost orders, no more disgruntled customers. The only drawback is that the interoffice courier will have to take up a new trade.

THE HUMAN FACTOR

Think of what network communications can do for the productivity of your staff! In many offices, the workers have little sense of the overall task to which they are contributing their efforts, or how the system functions as a whole. When the office is relieved of burdensome chores better handled by the network, the employee becomes a working partner within the office environment, with increased responsibility. This makes the person fully accountable only to his or her own actions—and to your customers.

Productivity is no longer measured by hours of work or items produced; it is judged by how well customers are served. Are they satisfied? Will they bring their business back? Are they willing to pay a premium for high-level service? To the extent that the answers are yes, your company gains an edge over the competition. A shift from paperwork to electronics can improve productivity, service to customers, and job satisfaction.

LAN IN THE FACTORY

Offices are not the only environment in which LANs can proliferate. Factory life is very agreeable to them. In fact, you might say that the concept of LANs was born of factory needs.

The impact of computer networks in the factory, however, has been grossly misunderstood. The emphasis has been almost exclusively on the production process itself, and a modern factory has come to be symbolized by the industrial robot, a computer-driven machine designed to replace the human worker. There is no doubt that without local area networks coordinating assembly lines, the robot would be little more than an expensive oddity.

Actually, though, the direct work of making or assembling a product is not where computer networks are likely to have their greatest effect. Direct labor accounts for only 10 to 25 percent of the cost of manufacturing, and the workforce engaged in such tasks makes up less than two-thirds of a factory's total employment. The major challenge is in organization, scheduling, and managing the total manufacturing enterprise. From product design to fabrication, distribution to field service, the complexity of the modern factory is daunting. In some plants, thousands of parts must be kept in inventory for hundreds of products. It is not uncommon for a metal part to spend 95 percent of its total construction time waiting to be processed. Indeed, the complexity of the operations has sometimes led to a situation resembling gridlock on the factory floor.

Thus, the productivity of a factory depends in large measure on the way the resources of labor, machines, and raw materials are brought together. Communications is the key word here. Direct coordination between management, labor, and vendors can be the only viable answer to profitable manufacturing. Local area networks have the ability to support the complex communications needed in this environment.

THE LAN PROMISE

The utilization of technological innovation often evolves in two stages. In the first stage, the innovation is exploited to perform better the tasks that were already being performed. This is the level at which most of us view networking.

In the second stage, though, new applications are discovered which could not be reasonably performed or foreseen prior to the innovation. Local area networks stand at the threshold of this second stage. While there is still much room for creative application of networks in everyday situations, the promise of the local area network lies in the identification of new applications that will forever change our concept of networks.

An office automation survey conducted by Omni Groups, Ltd., revealed that the use of local area networks to connect word processors, personal computers, printers, and even mainframes will proliferate in the next two years. It is estimated that by 1990 between 40 and 50 percent of all American workers will be making daily use of electronic-terminal equipment. Some 38 million computerized workstations of various kinds are likely to be installed by then in offices, factories, and schools. And these 38 million voices need to be heard.

3

WHERE DO I START?

Selecting a communications network is no simple chore. There are at least 70 different networks on the market, each touting its advantages above the rest. The market is further muddled by the fact that networking vendors often try to compare their products to other networking products by lumping them all together, when in fact they may not be comparable at all. You must sort the apples from the oranges.

Your first step is organizational. The key word is definition. Analyze and define your needs before going shopping. With the wide range of LANs that are available, there is a network to fill virtually every conceivable application. All you have to do is find the one for you.

The selection of a communications network takes a little expertise in both technology and management. I will break them into separate sectors as best I can, but the two must be considered as a whole.

ORGANIZATIONAL CONSIDERATIONS

Network administration and control is a subject often ignored in network considerations. A clear understanding of what you expect the network to do must begin with administration and control. What job assignments are being filled now and who is doing them? Look at the assessment in light of the ideal solution. That is, is the job really necessary, or could it be assigned to another person, given the right tools? How many jobs would be

11

directly affected by a communications network? Indirectly? When asking yourself these questions, don't overlook the obvious. Just because you have a function that has always been done efficiently the old way, and you can't immediately identify networking benefits, don't let it escape your perusal.

The next step is to forecast future requirements. Determine, preferably from existing records, recent rates of growth. Publicly accessible growth rates are often optimistic sermons intended for stockholders and board trustees, and in reality have little fact. Avoid them if possible. Keep a level head and use good judgment in your estimation. It is desirable to consider both the medium term, say, a year or two, and the long term of five years or more.

Now put all these facts together and determine who will be in control within your time frame. Will the network allow you to expand responsibilities and permit decentralized control, or is it desirable to keep it centrally controlled?

Centralization is the characteristic of organizations that are hierarchically structured, with a formal chain of command. You might even say, bureaucratic in approach. Certain organizations may find this style of technology more acceptable because it closely parallels their own philosophies.

Decentralization, on the other hand, refers to organizations that are not very hierarchically structured, have fewer chains of command, allow for more local autonomy, and are not considered bureaucratic. If you feel this is the direction your company should take, then your network should reflect this policy.

While scrutinizing your situation, you should be on the lookout for these other considerations. Although they may appear to be technical at first, they really fall under the cloak of organization. Let's take **ease of installation,** for instance. Just how do you plan on routing the cables required for the network? Do you intend to use existing facilities, or is it possible that the south wall is destined to be revamped in a year or so? Perhaps the two programs could be done simultaneously at savings to both. Do you plan on moving soon, or will the network be temporary?

Which brings up the issue of **flexibility**. How often in the last year has the office furniture been rearranged? Will this pose a problem with network connectivity?

WHERE DO I START?

Do you expect to be adding new positions soon? **Expandability** should be high on your list of priorities. Will the network provide for your anticipated expansion?

Management and control, flexibility and expansion, ease of installation. Technical? Perhaps, but a decision to be made at the management level, not after the system has arrived. Above all, make the network conform to your particular needs, rather than you catering to its whims.

PERFORMANCE CONSIDERATIONS

This part of the process is a little more technical than the last, but it still falls under management guidelines. A case in point is the size of the network. Sure, you can turn this chore over to an engineer or the salesperson. But do they know all the facts?

Networks come in all sizes, with two factors involved. First, there is the physical aspect of the area to be served. For this you will actually have to go to the vendor. Only the vendor knows how large an area the network will serve. There are several factors to be considered, including signal attenuation, propagation delay, and overall design—none of which should be your concern. All you actually need to know is whether or not the vendor's network will support your area.

Network size is also determined by the number of users it will support. This must be your determination. When considering this number, bear in mind future expansion plans. Will you be needing more capacity in the near future, or will subnetworking (Chapter 12) be a wiser choice? It is also important to focus on the expansion pattern rather than on actual numbers when making this determination. A few terminals or workstations here or there will have less impact than will a new service, such as electronic mail.

That is why speed is important. The number of stations a network will support is directly related to the amount of time required to send a message. Services, such as electronic mail, tend

13

to use more network time than casual communications because of the benefits offered. You will find that the amount of communications between individuals increases quite dramatically as they become familiar with the specific means of communication.

Data rates are judged on two considerations. The first is the actual pulse rate itself. It's obvious even to the technically uneducated that you can move 10 times more information at 10 Mbits per second than you can at 1 Mbits per second.

The second part of networking speed has to do with propagation delay. Many factors are to be considered in this figure, the least of which is the actual time is takes for an electronic pulse to travel the distance of the network. More significant is the management scheme, or *protocol,* used to gain access to the network. With most protocols, access time is a variable quantity controlled by network traffic.

Don't be fooled, though, into thinking data rates are the final word on network performance. Far from it. Many factors influence the throughput of data in a network, including the devices it serves. If you feed a 10-Mbit LAN with a 300-baud signal, you won't get top performance from the network, nor will you increase throughput by upping network speed. The network can only transfer data at the rate at which it is fed to it, no faster. If a 300-baud modem is your primary application, you are probably better off choosing a low-performance LAN, which costs less money.

Just keep in mind that speed costs money. If you want fast performance, be prepared to pay for it.

VENDOR SUPPORT

Perhaps the most critical decision to make, once you've set your goals, is to select a vendor you can live with. This selection extends to many areas and should be taken one at a time and weighed together only in the final tally. The main   objective, of course, is choosing a vendor that will support your equipment.

WHERE DO I START?

This support takes two avenues. The first is your immediate networking needs. Once you have decided upon the equipment to be interfaced and the services you require, it is a simple matter of sorting through all the qualified vendors and selecting the one most suited to your needs. If you intend on going with a single product line of computers and terminals, you may want to go back to the original manufacturer, who is increasingly offering local area networks for his products. If this isn't the case, or you are not satisfied with your manufacturer's past performance, you will need to look to third party vendors.

Here is where things get a little bit sticky. You must make judgements based on previous experience, which is not always easy. The LAN market is new, and new vendors are emerging every day—many without track records. In the past year alone, roughly 20 entrants have joined the IBM PC-compatible network competition. Obviously, there will be some fallout as the technology matures. Vendors with a reputation as a multi-product company have a better chance of satisfying your needs.

Going with a network that offers multi-product support solves some of the above problems. With computer products coming and going at a whim, it is reassuring to know that your network can support more than one manufacturer. Unfortunately, it doesn't answer the question of vendor reliability.

A good point to keep in mind when searching for a network vendor is to examine his future intentions. Companies which are more likely to have a solid base of operation than those who offer networks for a very narrow range of products and services, and they are more likely to be around when you need them. Nothing is worse than going with a system only to find out a few years from now that you are married to an orphan that locks you into a network from which there is no expansion or escape.

Finally, you should check into the technical services offered by the vendor. If you don't have a lot of in-house technical support, you will need to rely on the vendor. Some offer service contracts, others provide field support that works with your personnel. In general, no one vendor will stand out clearly from the rest, and the route you take depends upon your needs as decided from the information in this book and other sources.

OBSERVATIONS

Future LANs must serve a spectrum of device speeds and capabilities, including smart copiers, mail handlers, digitized voice exchanges, and teleconferencing mediators.

Also keep in mind that in the 1980s, a generation of workers with little exposure to, or knowledge of, computers will work alongside a generation that has grown up with computers. Data communications owners should take this into account when specifying LANs.

4

WHAT OPTIONS ARE AVAILABLE TO ME?

Before you can begin making decisions about networking parameters, though, you must be aware of your options. There are several choices to be made before and after you have determined your networking needs.

NETWORK MEDIA

One option you will be given is the type of network medium you can use to carry the electronic signals. The choices cover a wide range of technologies.

Of course, most will involve wires of some sort. Undoubtedly the most popular network medium is coaxial cable. Coax is the type of cable used to connect your television set to an antenna system, such as CATV, and it comes in a number of styles and sizes. Other networks are able to make use of less expensive telephone wire, generally referred to as twisted pairs. A thorough analysis of each is presented in Chapter 8.

Other media choices include fiber optics. For many reasons, fiber optics is the fastest growing medium for local area networks. As you will learn, fiber optics has many advantages over wires, and several networks offer it as an alternative to cables.

To round out your options, you will find networks that use infrared light, microwave beams, and radio frequencies to transmit network data. Not all networks, however, offer all choices.

SPEED

In many cases, the speed of the network will determine which network medium is used. As a rule, network performance can be gauged by its speed. The faster you can throughput data in a network, the more powerful it becomes.

Networks are divided into three categories according to their speed. Networking speed is usually listed as the *data rate*, and it is expressed in bits per second. Sometimes you will see data rates expressed as *baud*. Don't be confused by the jargon, though; bits per second and baud rates can be used interchangably.

Low-speed networks are typified by data rates that are less than 1 million bits per second (1 MHz). Medium-speed networks begin at 1 MHz and extend to 10 MHz. You will find that the majority of networks on the market today fall within these two categories. You may already be familar with some of them, such as Ethernet or Arcnet. We will be reviewing the particulars of these networks later in the book.

On the high end of the scale are high-performance, high-speed networks. These networks operate up to 50 MHz and beyond. They are generally very sophisticated and quite expensive, which is understandable. If you are willing to make the investment in high-speed hardware, which in itself is costly, vendors assume you are striving for maximum overall performance. Consequently, they pull out all the stops and add plenty of frills, with few compromises made along the way.

Be wary, though, of judging a network's performance solely on its speed. Data rates are often mistakenly used as a guide for network performance when, in actuality, *protocol* is usually the limiting factor.

Protocol is the scheme by which the network is managed. Different protocols fit different network styles better than others. For a complete analysis of this complex subject, refer to Chapter 9.

WHAT OPTIONS ARE AVAILABLE TO ME?

TOPOLOGY

Topology, the overall shape of the network, has a lot to do with how efficiently the protocol is used. The decision to use one topology over another is determined by several factors. One is the environment into which the network will be installed. Some topologies are better suited to certain surroundings than others. Cost also plays an important part in the selection of a topology. When given a choice between two workable topologies, you may find that one is less costly to implement and maintain.

Basically, there are three root topologies: the star, the ring, and the bus. All of your exotic-sounding topologies are merely specialized versions of one of these three topologies. Topology, which is probably the most discussed of all network parameters, is fully covered in Chapters 5 through 7.

Of more consequence than the topology itself, however, is the way the network uses the topology to convey messages. There are two ways of doing this.

The first is the *sequential network.* In a sequential network, a signal is passed from one station (or *node*) to the next in consecutive order. Think of a bucket brigade, in which a pail of water travels the length of the line by passing through one hand after another. In a similar sense, sequential networks require each node to process the signal, rejuvenate it, and retransmit it to the next node in line.

Broadcast networks, on the other hand, have the ability to talk to all nodes at the same time. This technique is similar to the way a radio station sends its messages across the airways. The information is broadcast for all to hear, and each individual node must decide which messages to process and which to ignore.

Whether a network is sequential or broadcast is decided by the topology and, to some extent, by protocol. Although there has been much debate as to which is better, there does not appear to be a clear-cut winner. Each method has its advantages and disadvantages, and the application determines what is better and what is worse.

19

SERVICES

The number of possible network applications is currently large and will continue to grow as both manufacturers and users become aware of the network's potential. It is clear, however, that any network which hopes to satisfy all the demands of modern business must provide certain basic services.

Communications, of course, is the chief service provided. But it can take many forms. In the office you may find it as electronic mail or database storage. Shared word processing and document preparation are also useful services found in office networks.

In the more general sense, network services can be expanded to include FAX transmissions, video conferencing, and voice communications. As networks proliferate, so will the services they offer.

Ideally, the network and its services should be integrated into an interactive package. Integrated services refer to digital data, voice, facsimile, text, and visual information used within a system in such a way that one complements the other.

Unfortunately, the view taken by most vendors at the moment tends toward the discrete application of services rather than an integrated approach. In some networks, for instance, services are even in conflict and cannot be used together. Consumer demand, however, is slowly changing the situation, and integrated service packages targeted at both specific and general applications are emerging.

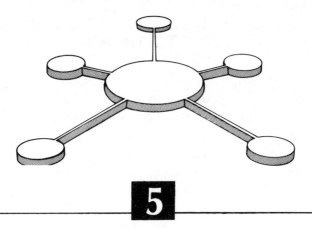

5

WHAT ARE STAR NETWORKS?

The first networking scheme to gain recognition as a local area network was the star configuration. Star networks have been around for quite some time and, probably unknown to you, they actually originated as a result of the telephone industry's reorganization.

When telephones began to proliferate in the late 1800s, they took the approach used by early computer networks: that of distributed networking. Young telephone companies wove intricate webs of phone lines between individual subscribers, often to the exclusion of some. In more than one instance, it was impossible to call a house across the street because the distributed networks, which grew as new subscribers came on the line, were mutually exclusive of each other.

The problems associated with this uncontrolled growth were so outstanding that in 1934 Congress adopted the Communications Act which gave AT&T absolute monopoly over the system, a position they enjoyed for 50 years. Their first priority was to untangle this web of confusion, created by duplicate phone lines and inaccessible substations, and replace it with one centralized exchange. Thus was born the *star network*.

STAR TOPOLOGY

Star topology begins with a central hub. At the core of the hub is placed a single intelligence. With the telephone company, it is an operator; in a computer network, it is a centrally located computer (usually a mainframe).

It is this concept of single-mindedness that gives the star network its superior performance. The central controller in any star configuration is an authority figure. This force, alone, coordinates and directs all network operations.

All subscribers to the network connect themselves to the central controller. In fact, the star network gets its name from the radiating pattern displayed by the spurs that connect the center hub to the outlying nodes. Unlike the distributed network, this is the only connection made to any node. Therefore, no longer does a node have to decide which path to take to reach a certain destination. There is only one route.

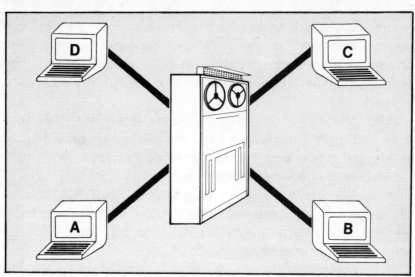

Star networks grew from the reorganization of the infant telephone industry into the AT&T concept of centralized control. Stars are characterized by radiating spurs, which emanate from a central hub to the outlying nodes. Each subscriber attaches itself to the central hub through a single link. At the core of the hub is an intelligence. In a computer network, it is a centrally located computer, usually a mainframe. Active stars require the central controller to be responsible for all network affairs, including message monitoring, traffic routing, and call forwarding.

WHAT ARE STAR NETWORKS?

Of course, this very simple topology allows for easy installation. Each time a node is added to the network, all you have to do is simply run a wire from the terminal to the main hub. And though this topology is not the most economical in terms of networking cable, it does lend itself well to expansion.

NETWORK OPERATION

Star networks are essentially sequential networks, since all communications must pass through the central controller for distribution. In fact, the operation of the central controller can best be compared to the duties of a telephone operator. To better explain network operation, we'll take an example.

Let's say that you are sitting at desk A and you wish to talk to the person sitting at desk C. You have a terminal at your desk and she has one at hers, neither of which can talk to each other directly. The assistance of the central controller is required. The communique begins with you ringing control central (operator) and giving the controller the address (phone number) of the computer terminal on desk C.

Star networks are managed a lot like the phone company of years gone by. At the center of the hub is a central exchange run by an operator. When placing a call from one node to another, you ring the operator and indicate the address (phone number) of the intended receiver. The operator then makes the connection, and you speak to your party. The drawback is that all communications must pass through the controller's hands, and when she's busy, it might take a while to put your call through.

The controller responds by first monitoring the network line for activity, then proceeds to ring terminal C. If terminal C is able to respond to the call, the link is established and you can communicate with your party. In the event desk C is tied up and unable to respond, the controller receives a negative acknowledgment (busy signal).

You now have two options. You can either try again later, which is how the telephone company handles the situation, or you can instruct the central controller to take the message and forward it to terminal C at a more appropriate time. This message storing is known as *online storage*.

The central controller is responsible for all network affairs. It must monitor all incoming and outgoing messages, place calls, and forward messages.

PERFORMANCE

Consequently, the overall performance of the network is directly proportional to the performance of the central controller. Unfortunately, performance is also directly related to price, so it goes without saying that the initial cost of a decent star network is quite high.

To justify the high startup cost, the network controller (hub) and the main computer are often combined into one. This approach has the advantage that only one expensive component need be purchased and it can do double duty. In fact, this line of thinking eventually led to the development of time sharing, in which a large mainframe computer provides services to many terminals on a time-shared basis while supporting the network. This arrangement gives the user of a dumb terminal, a workstation with nothing more than a keyboard and video display, the same processing power as an expensive mainframe.

However, this approach is not without its drawbacks. While the computer is busy playing "operator," it can perform no other useful duty. This restriction limits either the performance of the network or the computer as a processor—usually both. In a network where many terminals access the network on a frequent basis, an expensive mainframe often succumbs to the mundane role of housekeeper, relegated to the tasks of taking messages and directing traffic. Precious little time is left for other chores.

Network reliability is also a concern. If the normal pattern of communication is not between one primary node and several secondary nodes, but is more general (communications among all nodes), then the reliability aspect detracts from the star configuration. The whole operation of the network is entirely reliant on the correct functioning of the central hub. Should the main computer fail for any reason, the network is down.

Failure of a node, on the other hand, is of little consequence. Removal of a secondary node from service has no effect on network performance.

An inherent disadvantage of the star network is that each and every node requires a separate link to the hub. This can become quite expensive when nodes are distantly spaced in the network. Even with material notwithstanding, the labor cost alone can run quite high as nodes are added.

VARIATIONS

Star networks fall into two distinct categories. There are *active stars* and *passive stars*. Active stars are by far the more popular and contain an active hub such as we have just reviewed.

The passive star differs somewhat in topology from an active star, in that *two* cables extend from the hub instead of one. One line is incoming, the other is outgoing. This configuration is sometimes called a *two-cable star network*.

Replacing the computer controller within the hub is a transformer called a *coupler*. The coupling transformer is a passive device that takes the transmitted signal from a node and splits it up and distributes it to each node on the network. Its function is similar to that of a cable splitter often found on TV sets to divide the signal coming from the antenna into VHF and UHF inputs for the receiver.

As suspected, the splitter is unidirectional. That is, the signal can only travel one way through the transformer coupler, and a transmission line for one becomes the receiving line for all other nodes. Thus, the reason for the twin cables.

25

Management of the network is governed by the individual nodes. Returning to our previous example, let's assume again that we want to convey a message from our desk A to desk C. Instead of ringing the central controller this time, however, we place the address of the intended receiver at the start of the message and broadcast the data package over the network. Naturally, all stations on the network hear the broadcast, but only one—node C—will respond to it.

Of course, this configuration demands that each terminal has the intelligence to manage its own affairs. That is, it must be able to originate broadcast messages and recognize data packages addressed to it. This will bring up the cost of the individual node, but that expense is generally offset by the elimination of a central controller. The passive star is particularly attractive for personal computer networks, since it needs no controller and is easily implemented.

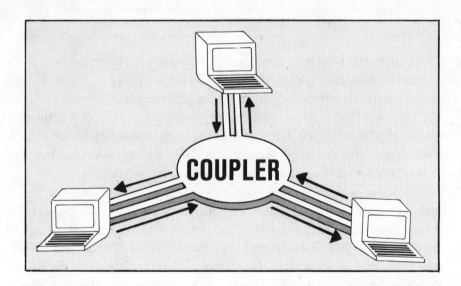

Passive star networks are a variation on the star theme. Imagine the operator being replaced by an electronic gadget that isn't quite smart enough to dial a phone number. Instead, it broadcasts your message to everyone on the network, hoping someone will recognize it.

Of course, this means every node must scan all messages as they are transmitted, looking for their names. Basically, it is a crude version of the bus network outlined in Chapter 7, but its low cost has ensured its application in a number of situations.

WHAT ARE STAR NETWORKS?

If you hadn't already noticed, the passive star is a broadcast network, whereas the active star is a sequential network. Passive networks are inherently more reliable than active networks. Only the complete failure of all coupling transformers (there is one per node) can bring the network down. Short of total disaster, this is highly unlikely.

OBSERVATIONS

Realize, of course, that the concept of a local area network was just unfolding during the earliest implementations of star networks, and many star networks were merely adaptations of telephone equipment. In fact, some computer networks in use today still employ PABX exchanges. In most cases, however, performance has suffered as a result. Recently, though, LANs have become more defined in their duties and responsibilities, and the star network has found its niche in the scheme of things.

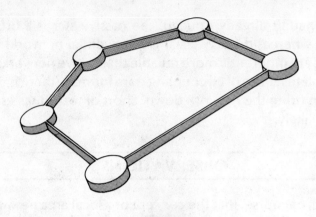

6

WHAT ARE RING NETWORKS?

The acceptance of star configurations as a local area networking scheme did much for the future development of LANs. Originally intended as a way to eliminate the rat's nest of wires created by the distributed networks, its greater potential was quickly realized by network users.

As a result, interest grew and it wasn't long before networking took on the guise of a computer science. Many users, though, disliked the fact of having to place an expensive mainframe computer in charge of directing network traffic. It is an expensive operator, to say the least, and more than a few people felt it hampered the network more than aided it. The introduction of the small, but powerful, minicomputer only served to reinforce this thought.

Spurred by these new developments, the networking community was forced to take a long, hard look at the evolving requirements for a local area network. They soon realized that the role of the LAN was maturing from that of an umbilical cord to a communications link. Designers agreed that a fresh approach was needed.

In an attempt to eliminate the central processor from the network, topologists developed the *ring network*.

RING TOPOLOGY

Ring architecture is essentially that of a distributed network with minimal connectivity. In other words, the wires have been straightened out and reorganized. The basic ring configuration consists of a *series* of nodes that are physically connected together via a continuous communications cable.

The ring is composed of a loop of wire fashioned into a circle. Within this circle are inserted the nodes for the network. To become a member of the network, the node must break the loop and connect itself first to one end of the break, then to the other, thus completing the circle once again.

Topographically, rings are easy to install in most LAN environments. All the loop need do is pass through the vicinity of the nodes. To tie into the network, the loop is broken and the node inserted. This is conveniently done using drop cables, one for the down link and one for a return.

This architecture is in direct contrast to that of a star, where every node is required to tread a separate path to the central controller. A star will need more—and sometimes much more—cable than a ring network.

NETWORK OPERATION

As before, the best way to understand the network is to actually put it through its paces. Using Figure 1 as a guide, let's follow a typical communique as it journeys around the ring. We'll assume that we want to get a message from point A to point D.

The process begins at node A, who originates the message and transmits it to node B. Node B intercepts the data and examines it. At the beginning of the packet is the address of the intended receiver, node D. Node B compares this destination address to its own and finds that they don't match. Therefore, node B regenerates the signal and passes it along to node C.

Upon receipt of the messages, node C also scans the heading for the destination address. Realizing that the message is not intended for it, node C forwards the data to node D. Finally, at

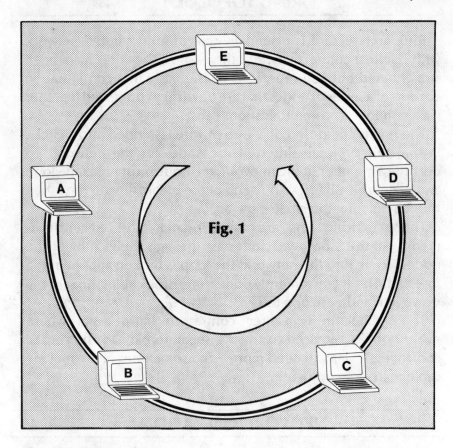

Fig. 1

Ring architecture is essentially that of a distributed network with minimal connectivity. In an effort to eliminate the central controller, the tangled web of wires encountered in a distributed network has been rendered to a single loop with each node attaching itself to the network on two sides. Because the network is sequential, a message journeys around the ring from A to B to C to D to E and back to A, with each intervening node examining and handling the data packet. At the heading of the packet is the address of the node for which the information is intended. Although the data may flow in either direction, most networks limit the flow to one direction only. In a unidirectional network, no routing decisions have to be made; the data is simply passed from one node to the next.

node D, a match is found and the data is assimilated.

Notice how the message progresses around the ring, in orderly fashion from node to node. Obviously, ring networks are sequential by nature. Unlike the star network, however, the sequence doesn't involve a central figure. Now that the network has been emancipated from the master-slave routine, each node is capable of making worthwhile contributions to the system.

In essence, the focus has been shifted from a processing network to a communications network in which everyone is allowed to participate. Workstation design can now be based on the immediate needs of the local user, rather than having to conform to a master plan.

When processing power or information requirements are greater than one node can fulfill on its own, the user has the opportunity of sharing the workload with other stations on the network. In fact, the ring offers the small-computer user the perfect opportunity for resource sharing while maintaining its separate identity. Such an arrangement with a centrally controlled network is both expensive and redundant.

Data integrity is of concern to ring networks. With the data being handled by so many intervening parties, the possibility that an error can occur is increased. In a star network, this is no big problem. Since each communication must pass through the central controller, it is relatively easy to spot an error. In a ring, however, the error can happen at any point along the way.

One way to insure data fidelity is to require the data to make a full circle before it is removed from the network. This rule forces node D to regenerate the message after digesting it, and pass it along to node E, who returns it to node A. If the information arrives at node A intact, with nothing missing or scrambled, it is assumed that the data was processed properly.

Another way to check the transmission is to have the receiving node remove the message from the ring and replace it with an acknowledgment. The acknowledgment, which contains the address of the originating node, travels from node D to E and back to A.

NETWORK RELIABILITY AND RECOVERY

As a sequential network, however, the ring is especially vulnerable to failure. A fault in any node or cable segment breaks the ring and brings network operations to an immediate halt. This type of failure is best compared to a string of old-fashioned Christmas tree lights: When one bulb goes out, they all go out. In any sequential string, this problem has to be reckoned with. To this end, network designers have made great strides. More than one technique exists for network recovery. The most basic is the bypass element.

Picture a node with a relay engineered into its transceiver circuit. This relay is placed across the input and output ports of the node in such a way that when the relay is de-energized, it shorts the two together. During normal operation, the relay is engaged, thus forcing the network signal to pass through the node in normal fashion. In the event the node fails, the relay drops out of action, causing the signal to be shunted around the defunct station and ushered to the next node, thereby preserving continuity. This arrangement also permits a node to be taken off line without disrupting the network.

Unfortunately, this technique can only protect the network from being brought down by a defective *node*. It can't correct for a broken cable between nodes. For that, other recovery methods are used.

In all cases, redundant cables are installed into the network as a safeguard against network failure brought about by a break in a link. Let's consider the various recovery examples presented in Figure 3. Each has its own advantages and disadvantages.

Figure 3a shows a simple ring with a gap between nodes B and C. In its present form, the ring is broken and normal communications are impossible. We'll use this example to demonstrate possible corrective techniques.

Technique 3b solves the problem by running dual cables between the nodes. The theory is that if one cable breaks, the signal can travel through the secondary line. It is the most straightforward of the recovery techniques and the simplest to implement, since both cables can be installed at the same time in the

WHAT ARE RING NETWORKS?

same space. However, it does have the disadvantage that whatever physical force broke the first cable (the kind of damage often encountered in remodeling) is likely to have an effect on the second. More than one carpenter has accidentally cut through an electrical conduit.

In method 3c, secondary cables are routed between alternate nodes, bypassing every other station. Switching circuits are then used to bridge the gap. In fact, more than one alternate route may be employed in the same framework. Unfortunately, the switching function often complicates the repeater, which must now test the waters before transmission and decide which path to take.

Technique 3d uses the dual-cable setup found in 3b. In this case, however, the signal forges a new path through the network when confronted with a failure. To make the path work, though, the network must be bidirectional. A break between stations is patched by having the signal first pass one direction through the network, make a U-turn at the break, and return by an alternate route. Essentially, we have overcome the defect by creating a small ring within the ring.

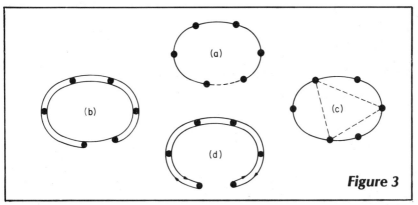

Figure 3

Network reliability is lowest of all topologies for the ring network. A failure in any one of the nodes or connecting links will bring network operations to a complete halt, as shown in part a. Several network recovery schemes have been devised to prevent total collapse. In example b, dual cables are run between the nodes. The theory is, should one cable fail, the signal can travel through the secondary line. Technique d uses a dual-cable setup similar to example b. In this case, however, the signal forges a new path by first flowing one direction and then returning in the opposite, making a turnabout each time the break is encountered. Example c solves both the problem of node failure and link separation by incorporating bypass cables that connect to every other node. In this scheme, network recovery is attained by using switching circuits to provide alternate signal routes.

All of the above cures demand extra cable and invoke extra cost. In addition, method 3c —which requires that the bypass links not be run alongside the original cable—involves even greater installation expense and possibly additional ducting. Node costs are also driven up when either method 3c or 3d is used.

RING VARIATIONS

In an attempt to solve the problems encountered in ring failure and recovery, the *star-shaped ring network* was born. In a star-shaped ring, the overall topology is a star, but the signal path is a ring. Each node communicates with the next node via a central wire loop, which is passive in nature during normal operation.

Should a fault occur in one of the nodes or the cables leading to it, however, the central hub would become active and circumvent the defective limb with a bypass circuit or relay. Operation of the control center may be manual or controlled by an intelligence such as a microcomputer.

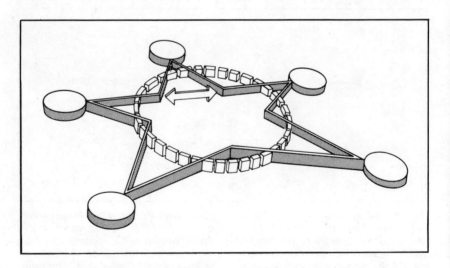

In an attempt to solve the problems encountered in ring failure and recovery, the star-shaped ring was created. In a star-shaped ring, the overall topology is a star but the signal path is a ring. Should a fault occur in one of the nodes or the cables leading to it, the central hub can maintain ring continuity by shunting the defective limb.

WHAT ARE RING NETWORKS?

This, in itself, makes the star-shaped ring very attractive for network use. But there is more. Star-shaped ring networks hold a distinct advantage over the routine ring design. The central hub doesn't have to be centrally located. The hub can be broken down into smaller hubs distributed throughout the network, usually as an interface between floors in a building. These satellite hubs are called *concentrators*.

Wiring concentrators provide both flexibility and reliability. Flexibility is provided by permitting each concentrator to service a small population. New nodes can be added to the network with a minimum of effort by simply cabling to the nearest concentrator.

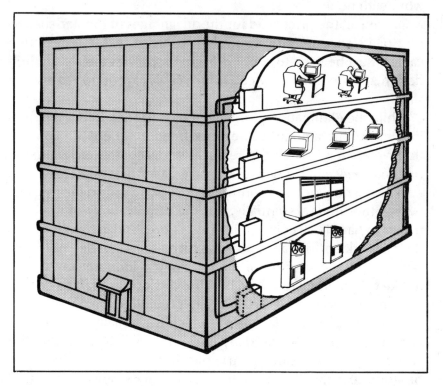

A variation on the star-shaped ring is often used for installing ring networks in buildings with widely separated work areas, such as one that has more than one floor. In this approach, the central hub is broken into smaller hubs called concentrators. Instead of the ring running the entire circumference of the building, connections are made only to the concen-trators, which are strategically distributed throughout the network area. To access the ring, a dual cable is simply run from the node to the nearest concentrator. As with any star-shaped ring, individual nodes or entire floors can be removed from the network through manipulation of the concentrators.

Reliability is inherent to the design, and is actually better in a concentrator design than it is with the centralized version of the star-shaped ring.

Naturally, each concentrator retains the capability of bypassing nonexistent or malfunctioning nodes at the local level. In addition, entire concentrators can be eliminated from the network in the face of catastrophic failure, where entire floors or buildings are involved. This is not an uncommon occurrence during a localized power failure that leaves most of the network intact but excludes portions. Selectively circumventing key concentrators permits entire sections of the ring to be removed from the network with no ill effects.

Of course, the price paid for the advantages of the star-shaped ring or its concentrator equivalent is higher cable usage. Two cables must be used to support each node; with the central hub design, this amounts to twice as much cable as required to install a star.

While the elimination of the central controller in the ring does imply a certain amount of network freedom, there are applications where it is desirable to retain a central controller yet use the ring topology. Such a network is called a *loop network*.

In a loop network, the controller occupies a spot in the ring like every other node. Essentially, it is the responsibility of the controller to handle all communications chores and generally gauge the network performance, making corrections as it deems necessary. With the exception of the topology, a loop network is not unlike the star network. And because the loop contains a central intelligence, you will often find that it is bidirectional.

Another variation of the ring, which is normally reserved for very small systems, is the *daisy chain network*. Daisy chains are commonly found in one-room applications, such as tying a printer or a disk to a single computer. The network employs dedicated lines, normally multiwire cables (Chapter 10), in parallel form to pass information from one peripheral to the next in sequential simulation. To pull this off successfully, though, data must be able to pass in both directions over the network. In fact, a daisy chain can be thought of as an open-ended ring with a Figure 3d patch over the ends.

WHAT ARE RING NETWORKS?

Unfortunately, the loop and daisy chain networks both experience the same vulnerability as any ring network. Unless recovery techniques are employed, failure of a node or link will halt network operations.

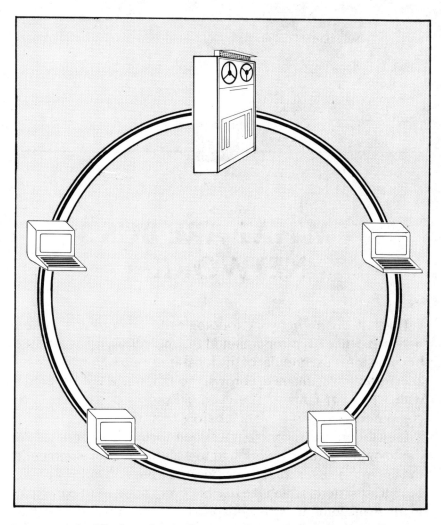

Loop networks differ from rings in that a central intelligence is placed in charge of the ring. This master node is required to handle all communication chores and generally gauge network performance. And though the controller is not physically at the center, all communications must pass through the controller for its perusal. In fact, most messages are either originated by the controller or intended for it. In a loop, the central figure is usually the only real intelligence in the network. The other nodes are often little more than dumb terminals.

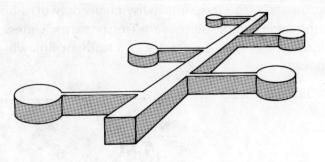

7

WHAT ARE BUS NETWORKS?

The last of the network topologies to emerge was the *bus network*. Since its introduction in the mid-1970s, it has grown to become the most popular of the local area topologies. Its appearance didn't raise many eyebrows, though, nor was it ushered in with any great fanfare. The eventual use of bus networks for computers was predicted long before their debut.

Even though bus technology was well documented prior to 1970, deployment of the network had to wait for the development of the microprocessor chip. This is because a bus network is a passive broadcast system, which means that every node must participate in the management of the network. Consequently, the nodes are more complex.

It wasn't until the advent of the microcomputer, with its proficient processing power and low price, that bus networks were even considered feasible. Since that time, progress on bus networks has advanced at a steady pace. In recent years, this technology has largely become the domain of the personal computer.

BUS TOPOLOGY

Bus topology is the most basic of all LAN configurations. It uses the absolute minimum topology to fill a geographical area while still retaining full connectivity.

The bus network is actually a specialized case of the star network. At least, that's how it began. Visualize a star network with its active central hub removed. In place of the hub, substitute a passive junction that physically and electrically binds the cable links together. This can be likened to the junction box used for electrical power.

Now, let's take our star pattern and stretch out the center connector so that it becomes a long wire. In the process of stretching, allow the node links to shorten and slide along the elongated hub. When we're all done tugging and pulling, we end up with a bus network configuration, as pictured above.

Notice that the nodes connect to the network through a tap to the main line. This tap is made parallel to the network bus. That is, the node cable is attached to the network cable in the same way you would splice two lamp cords together. A node can be attached to the network at any point along its length. At no time is the main bus ever cut. This is in direct contrast to a ring network, where the network must be broken every time a node is inserted. Of course, a continuous, unbroken cable provides better reliability.

Bus topology also lends itself very well to the geography of a building. It is much easier and cheaper to snake a single length of cable through a building than it is to run many individual lines, as required for a star network.

The main cable can be installed over corridors with drop cables leading to the LAN stations. Although ring networks can also conform to this type of installation, a return path is always required for each node, thus doubling the cable needed. Compared to a ring network, a bus network could save up to half in cable cost alone.

NETWORK OPERATION

Communicating over a bus network is totally different from talking over a star or a ring. The bus is a broadcast network, which places it in the same category as radio and television stations. Aside from the fact that LAN operation is license-free, the two behave similarly.

Let's take an example. I can best describe bus operation by comparing it to an old-time telephone party line. With a party line, several customers are tied to one pair of phone wires, with each sharing its resources. For the moment, ignore the central exchange, because we won't be placing any calls. We will only concern ourselves with the local group of subscribers, who laughingly used to refer to themselves as the ladies' sewing circle.

Being a member of a party line gave you certain privileges. If you wanted to know your neighbors' business, you simply eavesdropped on their conversations. Imagine a situation in which everyone eavesdropped all the time and all the phones were off their hooks at all times.

If Amy wanted to gossip with Edith, all she had to do was start talking. You can imagine it going something like, "Hey, Edith,

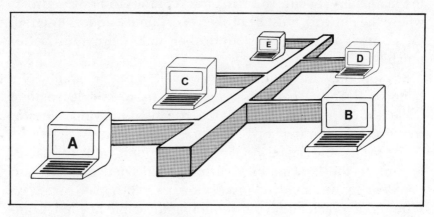

The bus is a broadcast network. In the operation of a broadcast network, the message is sent over the network medium for all to hear, the way a radio or television station broadcasts its signal to all listeners. To identify the recipient of the transmission, the message begins with the name of the intended receiver. A simple check by the individual nodes routes the message to its destination. Only the node whose name matches the address code pays any further attention to the broadcast.

have you heard..." Of course she heard, and so did everyone else on the line. But the point is that the message got through from Amy to Edith.

Now let's put this scenario into LAN context. The party line represents the main bus cable, the ladies' sewing circle members are the nodes attached to the cable, and the gossip is the data packets. Let's say you are node A and you wish to send a message to node E.

You begin by assembling a data packet. At the beginning of the packet you place the address of node E (Hey, Edith); the remainder of the packet is filled with the message and other protocol information (have you heard?). The data packet is then broadcast over the network for all to hear.

Once you begin broadcasting, each and every node stops and listens. They compare their addresses to the address heading on the packet. Only node E will recognize it, though, which prompts everyone else to go back to whatever they were doing, even if that was nothing. Node E, however, continues to listen and assimilate the data.

At the end of the transmission, node E will more than likely respond with an acknowledgment (a thank you). You see, unlike the other two topologies, there is no direct way of ascertaining whether or not the message was received. So the receiving node must broadcast an acknowledgment over the network to let node A know it was indeed received and understood. A negative acknowledgment means that part of the message was missing or garbled, a common occurrence in broadcast networks. The problem is resolved by retransmitting the data packet.

NETWORK MANAGEMENT

Like the ring network, the bus network is another attempt at eliminating the central controller. But that's where the similarity between the two ends. In a ring network, the network nodes aren't required to make any management decisions concerning data flow or network access. As it is a sequential network, these procedures are inherent to its design. The only requirement is that each node must take an active part in every transmission that comes down the pipe.

The bus network, on the other hand, is just the opposite. It is neither active nor sequential. It is a passive broadcast network that has the advantage that only those nodes directly involved with the communication have to participate. The other nodes can simply go about their business. Each node, however, must be able to recognize and respond to information intended for it whenever it comes across the network.

A passive broadcast network must also make data flow and network access decisions. This responsibility, of course, falls squarely on the shoulders of the participating nodes. In order to carry off this feat successfully, each node must possess the capacity to originate and transmit messages, recognize messages intended for it, acknowledge their receipt, and detect missing information. In addition to that, a node must also be capable of routing traffic.

Such sophistication doesn't come without its price. A bus network node has far more responsibility than either a star or a ring node, and prior to the introduction of the microprocessor chip, such a node was prohibitively expensive to build.

PERFORMANCE

Because it is a broadcast network, the bus has a greater potential for performance than any of the previous designs. In a star, network performance is limited by the central controller; in a ring, it is limited by node reliability and propagation delay.

Propagation delay deals with a host of factors, such as the size of the network and protocol used. Basically, propagation delay refers to the time it takes to get a message from one part of the LAN to another. This is usually controlled by network topology and management.

In a ring network, messages have to be constantly regenerated by each node as they make their way around the ring. This takes time at the regenerating station and results in propagation delay. Total propagation delay time is equal to the node regeneration time multiplied by the number of nodes the data must pass through before reaching its destination. If the intended receiver is to the immediate right, the data must pass through the entire ring before reaching its destination.

Not so in the bus network. In a bus, each node operates independently of the others, and messages are simply broadcast over the network for all to hear. The only delay encountered is the time it takes for the signal to travel the length of the cable, which is very small by comparison. This results in greater throughput for the bus network.

As a passive network, the bus also has excellent inherent reliability. A node can fail without disrupting the bus so long as the failure is in amode that presents a high impedance to the bus. A high impedance failure, which usually implies that the node has lost its ability to transmit or receive, will almost certainly disable the ring.

A perfect example is when power to a node is lost. Since the node can't talk or listen, it is essentially removed from the network. In a bus configuration, the network continues to function normally. Bus components must actually fail in a destructive way before they create a disruption.

However, not all the reliability issues favor bus topology. An example of a node defect that has a devastating effect on the bus is

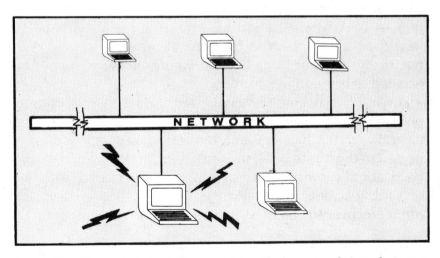

A most disturbing node defect is known as streaming or, as some like to put it, babbling. Streaming occurs when one station transmits continuously with no relief. When it occurs, the network medium is saturated with signal and the other nodes can't avail themselves of the network. This form of failure is not exclu-sive to the bus network; it can happen at any time to any topology. The bus, however, is more sensitive to its effects because there is no easy cure, whereas in a star or a ring measures can be taken to bypass the defective node without having to physically remove it.

known as *streaming* or, as it is sometimes called, *babbling*. This is a condition in which one station transmits continuously with no relief, thus preventing competing nodes from gaining access to the network medium. Anyone who has ever had a party line knows the frustration of having one user stay on the line seemingly forever, not allowing you to make your phone call.

Although streaming can occur in any network, the bus is most sensitive to its effects. In either of the other two topologies, the defective node can be bypassed internally. In a bus, however, the node must be silenced or disconnected physically before normal operations can resume.

Bus networks are also vulnerable to physical damage. A break in the main bus will usually stall network operations. Although it seems that a single break should partition the bus into functional half-buses, it is more likely to divide the network into two parts, neither of which can function properly.

The alternative, of course, is to run two cables—so that if one breaks, the network can be switched over to the backup cable. Unfortunately, this scheme has the disadvantage that whatever force damaged the first cable is likely to sever the second, which puts us back where we started. The problem of cable failure hasn't been totally resolved; bus network recovery techniques are not easily implemented. On the whole, network users have decided to live with the problem.

Physical damage to the network can also result from catastrophic disruptions, such as lightning and erratic power-line voltages. When this happens, one can expect all components connected to the bus to be destroyed. A ring network, on the other hand, doesn't have this worry. A power surge to one link will affect only the two nodes in immediate contact with the surge and, with proper recovery techniques, it doesn't pose a real network threat.

VARIATIONS

The bus network has a variation which is found extensively in the computer community. It is called a *tree*. The tree configuration is an extension of the bus in which several buses are joined together by active repeaters or passive splitters. This patching of network lines creates a characteristic branching effect, from which the network derives its name.

Trees come in two configurations: rooted and unrooted. Unrooted trees basically follow the scheme of the bus network we have described so far. Their branching, however, resembles the ramblings of a vine, with branching taking place at random points. The unrooted tree has no key components, and the interfaces are usually passive rather than active. Failure of a single branch—other than the main bus—doesn't normally disrupt the network. Ethernet is considered an unrooted tree topology.

Rooted trees, on the other hand, are characterized by having a unique control point at which some critical component is placed. This element can be anything from an active repeater to a central processor. Although bus topology was originally intended to eliminate a central controller, it is sometimes advantageous to employ one.

Rooted tree networks are commonly found in a classroom environment. In this situation, it is desirable to have one point of total control, that point being the instructor. The pupil, however, neither needs nor should have complete access to the entire

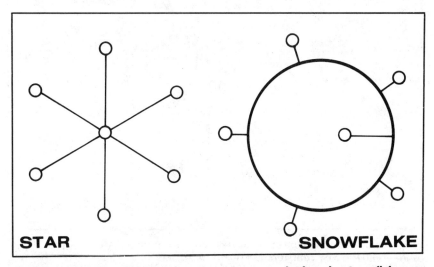

STAR   **SNOWFLAKE**

The bus network appears in many forms, sometimes unrecognized. Most common is the rooted tree configuration with a central controller. In fact, the star network can be seen as an adaptation of a rooted tree with a branch extending to every attached node. Snowflakes are another example of a rooted tree, though they are generally classified with ring networks. Close examination of most specialized networks usually reveals a bus network base.

network. The pupil's access should be to the instructor only, not to classmates. Tree topology permits this convention while supporting bus management.

Rooted trees can also be found in office buildings where more than one floor is involved. The tree provides the needed flexibility

A very common form of the bus network is the tree. The tree configuration is an extension of the bus created by joining together several smaller buses using active repeaters or passive splitters. This patching of network lines creates a characteristic branching effect, from which the network derives its name. Trees come in two configurations: rooted and unrooted. Rooted trees (pictured above), the more popular of the two, have a unique control point at which some critical component, usually a central processor, is placed. Unrooted trees have no such critical elements.

to carry the LAN services to several floors of a building or to the many buildings on a site.

The rooted tree can take many different forms. In fact, the star network may be seen as an adaptation of the rooted tree configuration with a branch extending to every attached node. Snowflakes are another special case of rooted trees, though they are generally classified as a ring network.

In either rooted or unrooted trees, the probability for network failure is increased where active elements are used, specifically repeaters. Failure of a repeater partitions the tree into two trees or buses. Unlike a simple bus, however, repeater failure doesn't normally bring the network to a halt. It will usually function as two separate networks, exclusive of each other, unless one branch is dependent on the other. This is the case when a branch of a rooted tree loses contact with the central controller, as demonstrated by the vulnerability of the star.

8

HOW DO I HOOK IT ALL TOGETHER?

No matter which network topology you select, networking boils down to the task of connecting one node to another. Whether you arrange them in a circle or in a bus, some form of signal conveyance must be used to bind the stations together.

There are several different media that can be used for carrying the digital information through the network. They range from the commonplace to the exotic. Some touch on the very frontier of technology, while others are as standard as time itself.

When choosing a network medium, you must keep several considerations in mind. They are price—and that means overall price including installation—expandability for future needs, ease of access, network speed, and maintenance.

TWISTED PAIRS

A very effective way to transport information from one place to another at a low cost is through a pair of twisted wires. Twisted pairs are no more than two ordinary wires run side by side. For electrical reasons, though, the wires are twisted together.

Twisted pairs are by far the cheapest of all networking media to buy and to install. The wires are generally small and easy to handle. They can be bent easily and conform well to tight corners, making it possible to run them along walls and under baseboards very inconspicuously. You must remember that in an office environment, aesthetics are as important as performance.

Access to the pair is also easily accomplished. If you are using a bus topology, access is as simple as removing a short area of insulation and splicing into the main line. You can access ring networks by simply cutting the loop and tapping into the open ends.

The bandwidth of twisted pairs is moderately high. You can expect decent performance at frequencies up to 1 MHz. This bandwith encompasses a wide range of potential devices, like file servers and low-speed modems.

NOISE

Unfortunately, the world we live in is just flooded with natural and man-made electrical noises. Noise consists of unwanted electrical sounds passing through the atmosphere.

These unwanted sounds come from such everyday devices as fluorescent lamps, air conditioners, typewriters, coffee pots, and the like. Most electronic equipment doesn't produce random noise unto itself, but what is desirable to one particular device is noise to another. Electrical noise radiates through the atmosphere in two forms, as radio-frequency interference (RFI) and as electromagnetic interference (EMI).

The point to all this is that exposed wires will pick up these stray sounds. Acting as a large antenna, the long runs of network wires intercept these signals and funnel them into the LAN. And unless they are somehow removed, they will mingle with the real signals, producing false data and reducing network performance.

Twisted pairs cope with this problem in a unique way. You can assume, and quite correctly, that when two wires pass through the same space, they will each pick up the same interference equally. So whatever noise one wire accumulates will be matched by the other wire.

Removing the unwanted signals is quite simple. We take the output from one of the lines and put it through an inverter. An inverter is an electronic amplifier that has the unique ability to change electrical signals by turning them upside down. What used to be positive becomes negative, and vice versa. If we now combine the inverted signal with our original signal, we can eliminate the noise. While one signal is going positive, its inverted counter-part is going negative. Since their magnitudes are identical, the net result is nothing—and total noise cancellation is achieved. It's like balancing the black and red columns in a ledger to achieve zero.

Okay, you say. So how do you keep the data signal from being cancelled, too? Easily. Unlike the noise, the original data was never put on the lines in equal proportions. There was always a voltage difference between them.

For instance, let's say that one line contains zero volts while the other line transmits positive five volts. These are common values in many networks. Even after passing through the inverter, we still end up with the same relationship between the two lines—one is still five volts in excess of the other. This would be the same as placing a value at the heading of a ledger column and never entering its equal on the other side. Only those signals which are common to both wires in equal amounts are removed by this process. Everything else passes through unchanged, and from this we derive our data signal.

However, this does have its limitations. A point is eventually reached where the background noise is so large that it literally swamps the data. That is why twisted-pair application is limited.

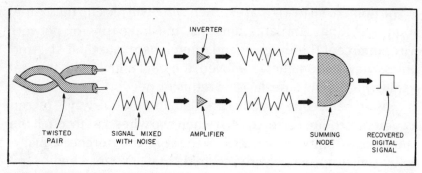

TWISTED PAIR   SIGNAL MIXED WITH NOISE   AMPLIFIER   SUMMING NODE   RECOVERED DIGITAL SIGNAL   INVERTER

A very effective way to transport data at low cost is through a pair of twisted wires. Unfortunately, the unshielded wires make excellent radio antennae and actually seek outside noises. This radio-frequency interference (RFI) is often many times greater than the digital signal, and the data pulses are easily masked by the noise. To remove these unwanted signals and recover the digital data, the output from one of the wires is put through an inverter, which changes the polarity of the electrical signal. When the two signals are recombined, the unwanted interference cancels itself out and a clean digital pulse emerges.

COAX CABLE

Obviously, noise reduction is best accomplished by simply stopping the noise before it enters the network, rather than taking measures to remove it once the signal has been contaminated. An effective solution is to shield the wires from the outside world by wrapping them in a metal shroud.

The simplest of these designs is the coax cable. A coax cable consists of a single conductor surrounded by a braided wire shield. To keep the conductors free from touching, the center wire is covered with an insulation called dielectric, over which the braid is wound. A plastic skin jackets the finished cable.

The inner and outer (braided) conductors carry the desired signal currents, with the outer shield going to ground. With the outer conductor grounded, any noise encountered along the way is intercepted and returned to earth before it has a chance to reach the inner conductor.

The bandwidth of coax is much greater than it is for twisted pairs. In fact, it is often in excess of 300 MHz. The dielectric constant of the center insulator, however, has a lot to do with frequency response. The type of material that is used and its thickness play an important part in the bandwidth. As a rule, the smaller the diameter of the coax, the narrower its bandwidth.

The dielectric constant also determines the characteristic impedance of the coax. The two most commonly encountered impedances are 50 ohms and 75 ohms, but you will run across some 93-ohm cable from time to time. The TV cable companies are the heaviest users of 75-ohm cable, while the military consumes the most 50-ohm coax. Most LANs specify a certain cable impedance for the network. Ethernet, for instance, uses 50-ohm coax. Although it isn't commonly encouraged, you can usually substitute one impedance for another on very short runs without much loss. However, I wouldn't recommend this practice for anything over 10 MHz.

Believe it or not, the length of the cable actually has more effect on the signal than does an impedance mismatch. No wire is without loss, and coax is no exception. As the signal travels down the coax, certain losses are incurred. This is due in large part to the dielectric absorption. The longer the run, the more signal is absorbed. A point is finally reached where the normal background noise is louder than the signal itself, and the two become indistinguishable. To counteract the effect, the cable is usually made larger.

Accessing a coax cable is usually simpler than accessing most network media, with the exception of twisted pairs. Coax is an established technology, one that dates back many years. It was first developed in the early 1930s as a means of channeling radar signals to and from an antenna. Since that time, the mechanics of coax have been standardized, and various connectors are readily available at very reasonable prices. In most cases, the coax is accessed by cutting the cable and inserting a T coupler.

A notable exception is the cable tap used for Ethernet. Ethernet specifies that at no time is the main bus to be cut, thus minimizing network signal loss and down time caused by bad cable splices. To obtain access to the medium, a special cable tap is used.

The tap is fashioned from a block of metal that is halved and which clamps around the coax. Into this metal block is inserted a finely threaded screw with a sharp, tapered point. The block aligns the coax so that when the screw is turned in, it pierces the outside shield and contacts the inner conductor. In fact, it is sometimes referred to as a vampire clamp. To keep the screw from shorting to the outside case, all but the tip and the threads of the screw is encased in Teflon.

COAX VARIATIONS

The metal shield is effective protection against both radio-frequency and electromagnetic disturbances. But even coax, if subjected to very strong interference, will not completely stop the penetration of undesirable signals. The answer is additional shielding.

Triax is a coax cable with an additional outer copper braid wound over the basic coaxial structure and insulated from the other two conductors. When this outer braid is grounded, it acts as a true shield—because it isn't used for a signal path—and protects the inner shield and conductor from noise. In order to be totally effective, however, the inner shield shouldn't come in contact with the ground and is operated in a floated state.

Like coax, triax has a wide assortment of standard connectors that are available as off-the-shelf items. Working with triax is only slightly more difficult than coax.

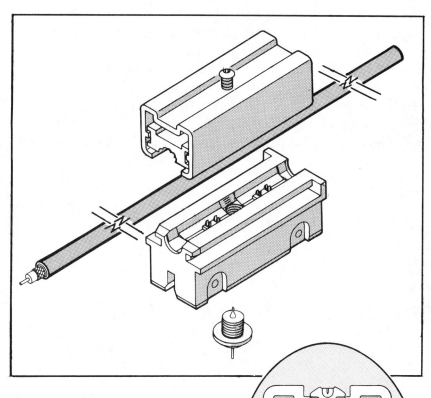

Coax cable, by far the most popular of the network media, is used extensively in LAN installations. Splicing into the coax, however, can sometimes be a chore. In most cases, the cable is cut and a T fitting is inserted. Ethernet has uniquely solved the problem with a special cable tap fabricated from a block of metal. Into this metal block is inserted a finely threaded screw with a sharp, tapered point. The block aligns the coax so that when the screw is turned in, it pierces the outside shield and makes contact with the inner conductor. All but the tip of the screw is insulated with Teflon to keep the signal wire from shorting to the shield.

SECTIONAL VIEW

But even triax is incapable of stopping the invasion of very low-frequency magnetic fields, like the kind produced by nearby power lines. No shield can reasonably deal with this type of radiation. Oddly enough, twisted wires can cope with it, even though they are susceptible to RFI interference. Combining the best of both worlds produces *twinax* cable.

In twinax cable, a pair of twisted wires is encased in a metal braid. As in coax, the braiding is grounded to prevent unwanted RFI interference from entering the pair. What little interference does get through—low-frequency EMI—is easily removed using the phase inversion trick we examined earlier.

Unfortunately, twinax is limited to 15 MHz of bandwidth due to the high transmission losses brought about by twisting the wires. The same feature that makes this technology so attractive is also

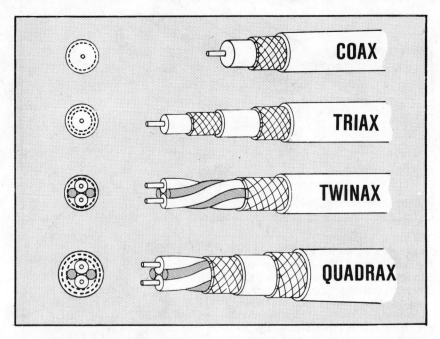

Noise reduction is best accomplished by simply stopping the noise before it enters the network. An effective solution is to shield the wires from the outside world by wrapping them in a metal shroud. This outer covering intercepts the unwanted interference and returns it to ground before it has a chance to contaminate the signal. A single-shielded wire is coax. For greater noise protection, the coax cable can be double-shielded, in which case it is called triax. Twinax and quadrax are single-shielded and double-shielded twisted pairs, respectively.

responsible for its shortcoming. But 15 MHz is still well within the range of most LANs. In fact, IBM makes extensive use of twinax cable in their ring networks.

If we were to take a twinax cable and cover it with a second copper braid, we would get quadrax cable. Like triax, the second shield is grounded and isolated from the inner conductors. This arrangement gives double RFI protection while maintaining good EMI rejection.

HELPFUL HINTS

Coaxial cable is a little harder to work with than a pair of twisted wires, and the problem is magnified as the cable becomes larger. Unless the cable is extremely thin (which limits performance), it won't fit behind baseboards or moldings. In fact, permanent damage can result if the radius of the coax is crimped too tightly. Once again, the thicker the cable, the larger the radius required.

As is usually the case, the coax is hidden above false ceilings and inside walls. Of course, this entails more labor, which leads to higher installation costs.

Maintaining coaxial cable is not difficult, but it is harder to accomplish when a cable is concealed behind a wall. Simply replacing a defective network link is often more economical than searching out and repairing the damage. To minimize failures, never splice in an inaccessible area. Defective splices account for the majority of cable failures.

When purchasing coax cable, be aware of what to shop for. First off, copper cables are best. Some cables use copperweld for the center conductor to increase its tensile strength. Copperweld is a high-strength steel wire with a copper cladding bonded to it, and its original purpose was to add strength to the cable when suspended between poles or pulled through conduit.

Unfortunately, copperweld increases the attenuation effects on the signal. Due to the high resistance of the steel wire, more signal is lost per foot than when pure copper is used. When selecting a cable for a long run, observe the insertion loss to ensure that your signal will reach its destination without incurring too much loss. If in doubt about attenuation, always go with the bigger cable.

Also be aware of the quality of the material you are buying. Manufacturers who offer coax at discount prices do so by skimping on the quality of the copper braid. Rather than a nice tight weave, they favor a loosely woven fabric that upsets the balance of the cable and allows noise to enter more easily. Conversely, poorly constructed shields also *emit* a fair amount of noise.

Leaky coax creates yet another form of noise pollution called *crosstalk*. Crosstalk occurs when the signal from one cable bleeds over to an adjacent cable. This is more common when two cables are run parallel to each other in the same duct. The only way to cure this problem is with proper shielding.

A good practice is to inspect the cable before buying it. As a rule of thumb, if the dielectric (insulation) is visible to the unaided eye through the braid without bending the cable, don't buy it.

Some cables are made without braid. In its place is a sheath of aluminum wrapped around the center core. Four to five strands of tinned copper wire accompany the aluminum to reduce the shield resistance. Don't be too hasty to buy this cable; it will only bring trouble. Although it may be okay in some applications, time shows that moisture in the air soon rusts (oxides) the aluminum away and turns it into powder. This often happens in as little as five years, and the only solution is replacement.

Where greater protection is required against vandalism, sabotage, rodents, or other high-risk conditions, armor covering can be applied over the cable. Be forewarned, however, that armor plating makes the cable less pliable and harder to work with. If flexed too many times, cable performance can deteriorate due to permanent cable distortion caused by the heavy armor cover. Factories, mines, buried cables, and top-security areas are but a few of the applications in which armored cable should be considered.

Cable prices vary widely, according to the type of cable involved and the manufacturing quality. Coax is more expensive than twisted pairs by about 50 percent. The improved varieties of coaxial design are also progressively more expensive, with armored cable being the most expensive.

APPEARANCE

In today's office, as much value is placed on aesthetics as on functionality. As with your own dress, demeanor is important. And you don't need to be disturbing the smooth lines of your room decor with unsightly networking wires and cables. Local area networks are to be heard and not seen.

As I have stressed in this chapter, cables can—and should—be hidden. Under moldings and behind baseboards is the most expedient approach. This is convenient and inexpensive, but practical only if you are working with two or three cables at a time—and provided they fit behind the trim.

But when multiple cables are involved, the bundle becomes much too bulky to hide behind a thin facade. Much effort has been expended in routing cables behind walls and above ceilings. In most installations, the coax is run through metal ducts mounted inside the wall. In future buildings you will see the trend swing to preinstalled networks—cables that are installed at the time of construction, as phone lines are today.

Stylish wall plates are also available to the network user to give the installation that sleek, finished look. They make attractive additions while providing convenience. As an added bonus, they make rearranging the office much easier. Simply pull the plug on one site and move everything to another outlet.

New forms of cable are being developed that will improve the unsightly task of installing networks in existing structures where it is prohibitive to break into walls. Already, flat "coax" cables that can be put under carpets have been introduced.

FIRE SAFETY

Hiding wires behind barriers is not without danger. Quite often, the rapid spread of flames from a fire can be attributed to the wicking properties of wires and cables buried deep within walls and ceilings.

By their very nature, networks are widespread, demanding that network cables be strung throughout an entire building. Oftentimes builders or remodelers simply shove them into wall hollows or drape them across ceiling supports, not realizing that these cables, once ignited, could spread fire to wherever they are routed. Vertical runs are especially susceptible to rapid spreading.

Furthermore, the burning wires cannot be observed, nor will smoke detectors be triggered until too late. And sprinklers are less than useless in this situation because heat is required to trigger them. By the time the heat from a wall fire is sufficient to set off the sprinklers, the entire building is usually engulfed.

At present, the only protection from this scenario has been to install the wires inside metal conduit. However, this practice is both expensive and not completely foolproof. Smoke from smoldering plastic wires inside the duct can be just as dangerous, if not more so, than the flames themselves. To make matters worse, due to the lack of accessibility, the fire is next to impossible to extinguish using conventional firefighting methods.

Recently, though, flame-retardant cables have made their appearance. Using TFE or FEP materials, these newer cables are nonflammable, low-smoke-producing, and approved for open installation. The cable may be more expensive to buy than standard cable, but the elimination of the metal ducts and the possible reduction in fire insurance premiums could more than make up for the initial outlay.

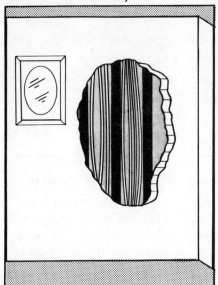

Although aesthetics are as important as performance, burying wires deep within the recesses of a wall is not without its dangers. Once ignited, network cables can spread fire to all parts of a building. Vertical runs are particularly susceptible to rapid spreading. Furthermore, burning wires aren't readily observed and pose a problem for smoke alarms and sprinklers.

FIBER OPTICS

In recent years, fiber optics has made considerable inroads into the communications field. Fiber optics is an extremely high-performance medium that has found widespread appeal in both telecommunications and local area networks. And even though it is still in its infancy, fiber optics is the preferred choice for LAN.

Basically, fiber optical communications consists of a single strand of glass "wire," about the size of a human hair, through which information is channeled. At one end of the flexible glass rod is a light source, like a laser or light-emitting diode (LED); at the other end is an optical detector. Light passes through the fiber tunnel to emerge at the other end. Information is carried over this beam through modulation of the light source.

As a result, fiber optics has many advantages, not the least of which is extremely wide bandwidth. In fact, it demonstrates a bandwidth that is 25 times greater than coax cable. And because fiber optics uses light instead of electricity for its medium, it is totally immune to external interference. Neither RFI or EMI disturbances can affect the quality of the optical signal, no matter how strong the force may be. Consequently, fiber optics needs no special shielding to ward off interference.,

Another strong selling point of fiber optics is network security. Due to the very nature of optical communications, it is virtually impossible to illegally tap into the fiber and intercept sensitive information without the tap being detected, thus making fiber optics ideal for high-security applications. Fiber optics also has a very high safety factor. There is no way a fiber can produce or (receive) an electrical spark that could damage equipment or start a fire, making fibers very attractive for hazardous environments.

Unfortunately, the very attribute that makes fiber optics so attractive is also the reason its progress has been slow. Good optical coupling and alignment are essential if good light transfer is to take place. Consequently, specially designed fittings and connectors are necessary, fittings which are both expensive and not easily handled by the average technician. So as not to be discouraged, though, you should know that reasonably priced connectors do exist and that qualified personnel can be found for those who wish to follow this route.

59

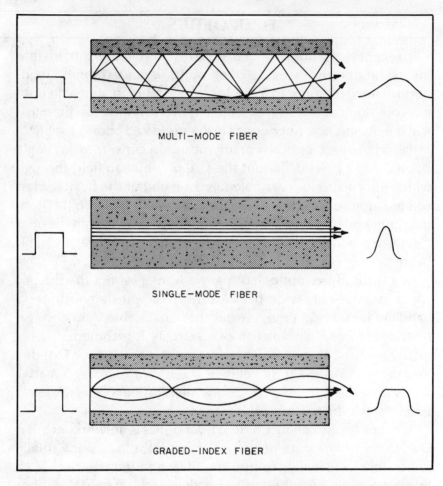

MULTI—MODE FIBER

SINGLE—MODE FIBER

GRADED—INDEX FIBER

Fiber optics is fast becoming the preferred choice for LAN media. In addition to being virtually immune to RFI and EMI interference, it also provides excellent security protection. Fiber optics is capable of extremely wide bandwidths. In fact, it demonstrates a bandwidth 25 times greater than coax cable. Basically, fiber optical communications consists of a single strand of glass "wire" about the size of a human hair, through which data is sent over a beam of light. The light travels through the glass fiber using the principles of index refraction. The fiber itself is made up of a silica glass that has a characteristic refractive index. Over this is bonded a thin cladding of silica glass with a higher refractive index. At the interface of the two glasses, a mirrorlike barrier is formed. When light is piped through the optical rod, it is reflected off this interface and ricochets down to the fiber to emerge at the other end. Glass fibers come in three different grades. The multimode step-index fibers are the most common and the cheapest. Single-mode fibers are very rigid and extremely thin; they find widespread application in telephone communication. Multimode graded-index fibers are the preferred choice of LAN applications, but they are more expensive than either of the other two. Signal distortion caused by light dispersion is a problem with fiber optics, and differs with the fiber construction. Depicted above are the input waveforms and their resultant output for the three fiber grades mentioned.

HOW DO I HOOK IT ALL TOGETHER?

Fiber optics, at present, is normally confined to sequential communications, with the data flowing in one direction only. This, however, doesn't really pose a problem. Most ring networks are designed to be unidirectional, anyway, and fiber optics fits comfortably into the scheme of things. Fiber optics has also been used successfully with passive star networks such as Ungermann-Bass' Net/One local area network.

Presently, fiber optics is more expensive than either of the other two media, twisted pairs or coax. However, optical fibers are still young, and as the technology matures you can expect a reduction from current prices. There is little doubt that, in time, fiber optics will be the technology.

INFRARED

Like optical fibers, infrared communications is fast invading the communications community. Unlike the previous media, however, infrared is absolutely wireless: No connecting wires or fibers are needed.

Infrared communications is very much like radio in that the signal is radiated into space and intercepted by an infrared receiver. The infrared frequencies lie well above radio and television frequencies and just below visible light, making infrared invisible to the eye.

Recently, infrared communications has come into the limelight with IBM's introduction of the PC*jr*. IBM has adopted this technology to make the PC*jr* keyboard totally detached from the computer itself. Inside the keyboard is an infrared transmitter that scatters infrared radiation about the room. The computer houses a sensitive infrared receiver that picks up this broadcasted light and turns it back into electrical signals that feed the computer's input. With no wires to bind you, you have complete freedom of movement while still maintaining full contact with the computer.

In the office, infrared links are used to tie various pieces of office equipment together. Operating in a bus configuration, an infrared signal is transmitted into the office space to be received by the other nodes in the network. Generally, the ceiling is coated with a highly reflective paint to minimize the loss incurred when

61

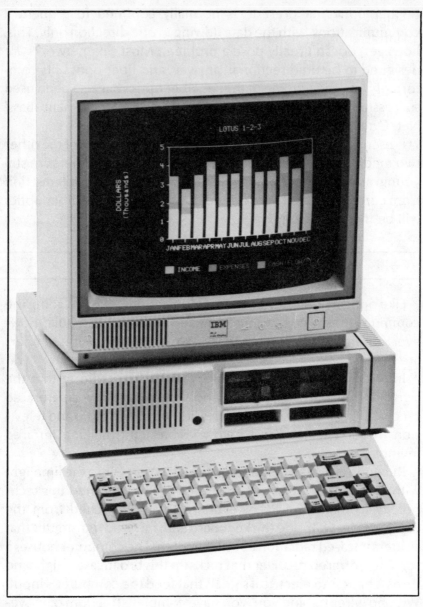

Recently, infrared communications has come into the limelight with IBM's introduction of the PC jr. Infrared communications is similar to a radio broadcast, but the frequencies involved lie just below visible light and well above radio frequencies. IBM has embraced this technology to make the PC jr keyboard totally detachable from the computer itself. Inside the keyboard is an infrared transmitter that scatters invisible light about the room. The computer contains a sensitive infrared receiver that picks up this broadcasted light radiation and turns it back into electrical signals that feed the computer's input. The PC jr permits you to walk about a room untethered as you issue commands and enter data.

the light bounces around the room. Placing office equipment in an infrared environment is a snap. You have absolutely no restrictions other than the necessity of intercepting the infrared rays.

Infrared can also find application outside the office. When a link must be established between nonadjacent buildings, the frequently sought solution is to string a cable between them. However, this is not always practical—or desirable. When the network has to cross public or privately owned property, things get a bit sticky—especially when it comes to digging up sidewalks. Permission has to be obtained, and in many cases an annual fee or assessment must be paid for the privilege.

With infrared, the task is made much simpler. A transmitter is placed at one site and aimed toward a receiver at the other. The information modulates the infrared source and beams its message across the distance to the opposite site, where the receiver decodes the signal and places the data on the network. This technology has been proved reliable for distances up to two miles and more. As an added bonus, the technology doesn't require FCC permits, as do radio and microwave links.

9

WHO MANAGES THE NETWORK?

Building a local area network is something like starting up a new assembly line. You need to choose the right equipment for the job and position it for the most efficient operation. In a similar fashion, you need to select your parameters carefully for a local network.

Obtaining all the right pieces and putting them together is only half the battle. Sure, we have the machinery (LAN) and the personnel (nodes) to use it, but we still need a manager to coordinate the effort. After all, an assembly line can't run smoothly if the manufacturing steps are out of sequence, and neither can a LAN.

In a network, management amounts to the allocation of network time, which is the only commodity the network has to sell. Local area networks are unique in that only one communication channel is available for all users, and it must be shared. This is not unlike a CB radio where more than one person competes for the privilege of the wavelength.

This raises many questions. Who gets to use the network first, and for how long? Who has access to it next? Does any one station have priority over the others? To settle these issues, someone has to be put in charge of the situation. Several schemes have been devised for management of LAN time. Some protocols are simple, others are more sophisticated. Let's look at the options.

CENTRAL CONTROL

The most obvious management solution is to assign one person the job. One controller conducts all network business, including operations, time management, and traffic control.

This arrangement is best suited to networks that already have a central controller in their scheme. The star network is a perfect example of this type of arrangement. Other networks that lend themselves well to this design are loops (rings) and rooted trees (bus). Generally, you have two management schemes in this category from which to choose: interrupt and polled.

INTERRUPT-DRIVEN NETWORKS

The simplest form of centrally controlled network management is the *interrupt-driven network*. In an interrupt-driven network, no special effort is made by the central processor to service the needs of the nodes. If a station wishes to use the network, it must ask permission to do so by interrupting the central controller with a request-to-send signal. The controller responds by granting permission to the request and permitting the node to speak.

Priorities can be assigned to nodes using this procedure. When two or more workstations request access to the network at the same time, the controller has the option of selecting the one with the highest priority and making the challenging station wait. Each node is then serviced in turn as the network becomes available. If a station with a higher priority interrupts while a lesser node is transmitting, the controller can preempt the latter and give access to the new node. This clears the network for pressing communications.

As you can imagine, there are numerous variations that can be made to this theme. The requesting node can even assign priority values to the data at the time of the interrupt, thus giving a node the opportunity to override higher priority stations in certain situations.

Although interrupt-driven networks are by far the simplest and cheapest to implement, they suffer from access uncertainty and long time delays. When a node requests network use, there is no guarantee as to when the request will be granted, or that a node with higher priority won't steal away the privilege at any moment. During periods of heavy traffic, it is conceivable that a low-priority device could be denied access to the network altogether.

POLLED NETWORKS

In a *polled network,* the central controller is assigned more active duty. Instead of waiting for a request to use the network, the central controller scans the network and successively invites nodes to use the network medium.

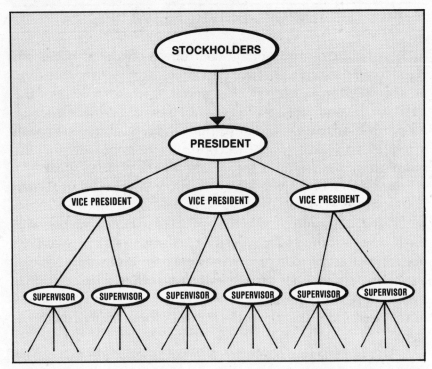

Without management, a LAN is little more than an odd collection of electronic hardware. The most obvious management solution is to assign one person to the job. Generally, this arrangement is best suited to a network that employs a hierarchical central controller in its topology, such as the star, the loop, or the rooted tree. Two elementary management schemes that are used with this theme include interrupt-driven and polled. Interrupt-driven management requires the nodes to request network time while polled management invites them to use the network.

WHO MANAGES THE NETWORK?

The commonest form of network polling is to query the outlying devices in a fixed rotation, the order of the polling executed according to a polling list. The controller completes a cycle when it has scanned the entire list and returned to the top of the roster.

Only the station with a current invitation can use the network, and only for a limited length of time as stipulated by the controller. If the polled node has a message to send, it is given access to the network. If it has nothing to say, the controller proceeds to the next node and queries it.

As with the interrupt-driven network, the polled network can be modified to suit particular network and priority needs. Very active stations may be polled several times within a single cycle. Inactive nodes, on the other hand, can be skipped over entirely during a cycle and polled on alternate or assigned cycles. For instance, if the node has only occasional communications, the cycle may be adjusted to poll that device every other cycle, thus allocating more time for the busier stations.

The frequency with which any particular node is polled can be adjusted by the controller according to the workload at the time and station activity. As node activity wanes, the controller gives less and less of its attention to that node.

This variable cycle is usually referred to as *roll-call polling*. Roll-call polling can even be extended to the point where a node is completely excluded from the polling process. To keep tabs on who is active and who is off the network, a broadcast poll is made once during every cycle, to which an inactive station may respond to make itself known.

Polled networks have the advantage of simplicity and fairness. Polling eliminates the long waiting periods experienced in interrupt networks by meting out time on a shared basis. This produces a network with a response time that has a known upper limit. A node waiting to send a message knows that within a certain time period the poll will return. This is highly desirable where time critical processes are concerned.

Unfortunately, polling suffers the fate of all centrally controlled networks. Failure of the central node halts network operation. The only viable solution to the problem is duplication of the controller, which in many cases, is prohibitively expensive.

TIME SHARING

The solution is to eliminate the central controller. Several of the topologies can give you that convenience, including rings and buses. But before we can eliminate the central controller other than physically, we must change our concept of network management. *Time sharing* is a decentralized management scheme that borrows its strategy from the polling networks.

In time sharing, the LAN time is equally divided into time slots. The actual timing period for a slot is determined by the size of the network (number of nodes) and the length of the message. In most instances, the time slot is a fixed period that is installed into the LAN at the time of its construction.

Each active station is allocated one or more of the slots. As its time slot becomes available, the node has the opportunity to transmit a message on the network. Distribution of the time slots is also considered during the construction phase. Allocation is based on the user's needs. If one station is to have priority over another, it can be assigned more than one slot per cycle, either consecutively or at predetermined intervals.

Unfortunately, time slotting is too rigidly fixed for most LAN applications. Besides being inflexible, it also wastes precious network time. If a node has nothing to say during its access period, the network silently waits for the period to expire.

Time sharing is one way to manage a network without a central controller. Time sharing gives everyone a chance at the network by dividing network time into equally segmented time slots. Each node is then assigned a time slot. When a node's time slot number comes up, it has full access to the network for a prescribed period of time.

SLOTTED RING

In an effort to reduce the idle time in the network, a variation to the time-sharing theme called the *slotted ring* was created. As its name suggests, it was originally developed for use with a ring network.

For data transfer, the slotted ring uses a series of message slots that are rapidly rotated around the network. Each slot is capable of storing a data packet. You might say a slotted ring is analogous to a string of railroad boxcars traveling a circular track. The boxcars represent the message slots; as each car passes before a node, the node has the opportunity of loading it with a message.

The slots are labeled with a binary code to indicate the status of the boxcar. A "full" slot contains a message, an "empty" one doesn't. A station with a message to send searches the passing cars for an empty slot. When it finds one, it sets the marker to "full" and inserts its message as the slot flies by. Since there are several slots circling the network at the same time, more than one node may be putting a message on the network at the same time.

At the head of the data is the address of the intended receiver. All nodes monitor the address slots as they pass by. When a node recognizes an address as being its own, it reads the message. After reading the message, the node attaches an acknowledgment to

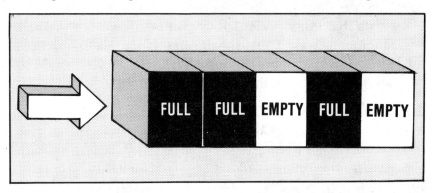

A variation of the time-sharing theme is the slotted ring network. As its name suggests, it was originally developed for use with a ring network. The slotted ring is analogous to a string of railroad boxcars traveling a circular track. Each car represents a message slot in which data can be inserted. A station with a message to send searches the passing cars for an empty slot. When it finds one, it inserts the message as the slot flies by. The most famous slotted ring network is the Cambridge Ring.

the end of it. The data packet then continues on its way around the network.

When the data slot with its acknowledgment tag returns to the originating node, the message is removed and replaced with an empty marker. The slot is now available for use.

To prevent one node from hogging all the available transmission capacity, the sending station is not allowed to reuse a slot from which it has just removed data. At least one cycle must pass before it may access that slot again. Probably the best known slotted ring network is the Cambridge Ring developed by Cambridge University, England, in the mid-1970s.

In certain slotted ring configurations, the receiving station may be required to remove the message itself and set the empty flag. This is particularly attractive because the same slot may be used more than once per cycle. The network is thus permitted to transfer data at a rate in excess of the actual rotational speed since a data packet doesn't have to come full circle.

The price paid for these advantages is that the slotted ring is very inefficient in its use of transmission capacity. As a general rule, a full 60 percent of the total bandwidth is taken up by control bits, leaving a scant 40 percent for actual data.

Furthermore, this technique is not completely decentralized. One node must be selected to generate the slots initially and continually review the information contained within them, removing data that other nodes fail to capture after more than one pass. If someone wasn't put in charge of this housekeeping chore, the network would soon clog up with useless data created for nonexistent addresses either in error or by node removal.

TOKEN PASSING

A very promising management scheme called *token passing* surfaced sometime between the late 1960s and the early 1970s. This mechanism was originally devised for use on a physical ring, but it has found widespread application with all network topologies. It, too, is a decentralized protocol.

Token passing is really a distributed form of roll-call polling, where stations are invited to use the network. Network use is determined by an electronic tag called a *token*. There is only one token in the network, and only the node which possesses it has the right to full advantage of the network medium.

So that everyone has an opportunity to use the network, the token is a circulated item. Once a node receives the token, it is permitted to use the network for a prescribed amount of time. When the node has finished sending its message or its time has expired, the token must be relinquished to the next node in the network.

For example, let's say that station 19 has the token through whatever fate delivered it into its hands. Node 19 now has exclusive use of the network. When it has finished, node 19 gives the token to station 53 (because it has been programmed that way). This now gives station 53 access to the network.

Should station 53 have nothing to say, however, it would simply pass the token to the next node without delay. And so the token goes around the network in a circular fashion, giving every station opportunity to use the LAN as its turn comes up. The last node on the line returns the token to the first node, and the cycle begins over again.

Token passing is a distributed form of roll-call polling, where stations are invited to use the network. Network access is determined by an electronic tag called a token. The token is a circulated item that is passed from station to station. Only the node in possession of the token has the right to talk on the network. Once a station has finished its conversation, it forwards the token to the next node in the network. Arcnet has become the de facto network standard for token-passing protocol.

ARCNET

Arcnet, developed and licensed by Datapoint, is a token-passing network that has become a *de facto* standard among LANs. Arcnet actually began as a physical star network that was treated as a broadcast bus. But the line dividing a passive star from a bus network is faded at best, and Arcnet has found application in most network topologies.

Datapoint likes to refer to Arcnet as a *modified* token-passing network. Arcnet is modified in the way it controls distribution of the token. Up to this point, we have not run into a network management scheme in which the removal of a node is of much consequence. In fact, some of the methods employed so far even encourage the practice (like roll-call polling).

In a token-passing network, however, node removal is a problem. Deletion of a node from the network amounts to no less than loss of the token. After all, what good is a perfectly thrown forward pass if nobody's there to catch it? A token passed to a nonexistent node is as good as lost.

To prevent the loss of a token during normal operation, Arcnet requires that the node passing the token monitor the LAN for activity. A successful exchange is always followed by a burst of network activity generated by a data packet or the subsequent forwarding of the token. If the network remains silent for more than 78 microseconds after the token is passed, the originating node assumes that the token has been lost and reclaims possession of it. A search is then made to find a station capable of accepting the token.

To illustrate the point, let's assume that node 19 has a token and passes it along to workstation 53. Now, if station 53 has been removed from the network, or shut down, it can't acknowledge receipt of a token. This becomes apparent to node 19 when the 78-microsecond timing period expires and nothing has happened. Node 19 now takes charge of the token and increments the destination address by one to 54. And the token is sent to station 54. Failure of 54 to respond forces node 19 to advance the destination code to 55 and try again.

WHO MANAGES THE NETWORK?

The process continues until, finally, a node is found that can accept the token and acknowledge its presence. This new address is permanently recorded in node 19, and each time it receives the token thereafter, it forwards it to the new address.

Adding a node to a token-passing network, however, is somewhat more complex than removing one. Addition of a node requires the entire network to be reconfigured. Arcnet approaches this responsibility with a unique network-reconfiguration scheme.

Let's suppose that station 53 wants to get back on the network. To do so it simply broadcasts a reconfiguration burst pattern. What this does is scramble the network and erase the token's destination address for every node on the network. Immediately following the reconfiguration burst, each workstation starts a timeout clock. The length of each node's timeout period is determined by its address. The node with the highest address times out first and gains possession of the token.

It is now the duty of that node to start the token-passing process. The node does this by broadcasting the address of the lowest known workstation and asking if anyone listening can answer the call and accept the token. If unanswered, the node increments to the next address and makes a similar query. When a recipient is found, the token is passed. The forwarding address is then stored in the memory of the initiating node.

Each subsequent station receiving the token goes through the same procedure, beginning with its own address plus one and looking for the next node in line. When the token returns to the highest numbered node, the reconfiguration is complete. Once reconfigured, the network can go back to work, including station 53.

OBSERVATIONS

Token-passing networks have the advantage that little time is wasted in the management process. If a node doesn't need to use the token, it is immediately passed along to the next node. The transit delay time of the token depends upon how many stations take advantage of the network. As the workload increases, it takes longer for the token to return once it has been relinquished. However, there is an upper limit to the time that will lapse before its ultimate return, based on the number of nodes in the network and assuming every node takes full advantage of the token. This makes token passing very attractive in situations where response time is critical.

On the negative side, token passing does require a workstation with a considerable degree of intelligence, which is reflected in its price. In most instances, token passing is used with networks made up of personal computers and microcomputers as nodes. These powerful machines can serve as both network managers and workstations.

Another problem encountered in some networks is overhead time. If the network tends to be more fluid than static—that is, nodes are switched on and off the line frequently—much time is wasted with reconfiguration and node-searching procedures.

CONTENTION

The network management schemes that we have reviewed so far are carefully planned mechanisms that provide network access in a very logical and sequential order. Unfortunately, a node's need to communicate across the network is not so orderly and often comes at unpredictable times. In polled and token-passing networks, each station is required to defer transmission until it is authorized to begin by invitation. The only exception is the interrupt-driven method, which requires a central controller, making it unsuitable for unrooted bus use.

One very simple control strategy that has been used successfully for broadcast networks is *contention*. In a contention network, any node wishing to send a message simply does so. There are no controls or priorities to stop a node from seizing access to the network whenever it desires.

This is fine—if the network happens to be idle at the time. But you can't always expect that to be the case. There is nothing to prevent two nodes from transmitting simultaneously. Although it is certainly true that most communiques are just short bursts of data, and have a good chance of catching the network clear, it is inevitable that somebody's going to step on someone else's toes and walk across a conversation.

When this happens, a collision results and the receiving nodes can't make head or tail of the garbled mess. Of course, the transmitting nodes don't know what has taken place, as yet. They get a clue when the receivers fail to respond with the proper acknowledgment. If an acknowledgment isn't received within a reasonable period of time, the message is rebroadcast. And though a collision may occur again, the likelihood of its happening twice in a row is low. The more times a node transmits a message, the better the chances of getting it through unscathed.

Although this may appear to be a helter-skelter way of doing things, it does have a basis in fact. The method assumes that network traffic on the average is small and that the probability of a message getting through on the first try is pretty good. It also assumes that the bandwidth is relatively cheap and expendable and that the bandwidth wasted on collisions is a small price to pay for the simplicity of the scheme. Unfortunately, less than 20 percent of the total bandwidth is actually usable—18.6 percent, to be exact. The other 80 percent of the time the network is either idle or in collision.

RULES OF GOOD BEHAVIOR

- **LISTEN BEFORE TALK**
- **CARRIER-SENSE MULTIPLE-ACCESS** *(CSMA)*
- **BACK OFF IF COLLISION OCCURS**
- **LISTEN WHILE TALK**
- **CARRIER-SENSE MULTIPLE-ACCESS WITH COLLISION DETECTION** *(CSMA/CD)*

A simple, though effective, control strategy used successfully for broadcast networks is contention. In a contention network, any node wishing to send a message simply does so. This method is similar to the working of a CB radio. If you want to talk on the CB, all you have to do is push a button and start talking. To prevent two stations from broadcasting at the same time, though, a few simple rules of courtesy are observed. You always listen before talking to make sure the channel is clear, and if you do happen to walk across someone else's conversation, you back off and let that person finish before you try again. Contention networks abide by these same rules. Ethernet appears to be the de facto standard among contention networks.

CONTENTION RULES

To improve network performance, some basic rules concerning network access had to be established. They are often referred to as "rules of good behavior" for reasons that will soon become clear.

As you know, it is more polite and productive to wait for a conversation to end before speaking. Interrupting a person who is talking nets you nothing but scorn. This simple rule of courtesy, when extended to local area networks, changes the whole personality of the network.

Before a node can transmit on the network, it must first listen. If a conversation is in progress, the node must patiently await the conversation's completion before taking any action. This simple courtesy, Carrier-Sense, Multiple-Access (CSMA), greatly reduces the number of collisions and increases network efficiency beyond 50 percent.

However, collisions can still occur. If two nodes are waiting for the same conversation to end, it is very likely that both will attempt to capture the network at the same time, resulting in a collision. In fact, the heaviest concentration of collisions occurs immediately following a successful transmission. As network traffic increases, the probability of this happening also increases.

In the basic contention scheme, a message is transmitted to completion. This means a collision won't be detected until the node starts looking for an acknowledgment. This is a terrible waste of time because an entire data packet must be transmitted before monitoring even begins.

If the transmitting node were to monitor the network while it was talking, it could identify a collision as it happened and immediately halt transmission. Keeping the network as free as possible of useless data generated by collisions increases network utilization to over 90 percent. This management plan is known as *Carrier-Sense, Multiple-Access/with Collision Detection*, or CSMA/CD.

When a collision is detected, the competing nodes back off and go into a holding pattern before attempting retransmission. The amount of time spent in the holding stage is determined by an onboard timer. Unless the nodes wait different periods of time, though, another collision is inevitable. When competing nodes wait exactly the same amount of time they will always collide and the network will become deadlocked. A deadlock can only be avoided by giving each station its own unique waiting period, either permanently installed or using a random-number generator.

ETHERNET

Ethernet is a contention network that incorporates all the above rules for good behavior (CSMA/CD). Ethernet was developed by Xerox at its Palo Alto facility in 1975. Through a combination of vigorous mass media campaigns and low licensing fees, Xerox has

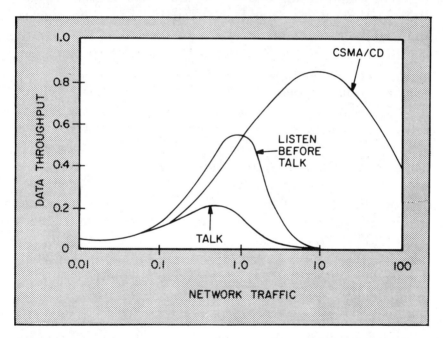

There is much debate about which protocol is better, token passing or contention. Each has its advantages and weaknesses. The biggest difference seems to be in the delay time encountered when trying to send a message. A comparative evaluation of the performance of Ethernet and a token-passing ring has concluded that though the former functions well under light loads, increasing traffic increases the number of collisions which, in turn, reduces network performance. The token-passing network, on the other hand, guarantees a maximum delay time, even in periods of heavy traffic. Ethernet has no such guarantee. It is even conceivable that a contention network could become deadlocked because the number of nodes competing for network time is so great that the network remains in perpetual collision; this does in fact occur, as illustrated above.

earned Ethernet the honor of becoming one of the two *de facto* network standards in the industry today (Arcnet being the other).

Adhering to the first rule, an Ethernet node must listen to the network and find it clear before it can transmit. Should the Ethernet inadvertently interrupt another conversation, the Ethernet controller contains a receiver that monitors the transmission as it is sent. The moment it detects an overlapping of pulses caused by a collision, it stops transmitting. An abort pattern is then broadcast, informing all nodes on the network that a collision has occurred, and the competing stations go into a holding pattern.

The time-out period is determined by a complex algorithm that generates a random number. This random number is plugged into the controller's timer. After the time-out period, the node again listens to the network for activity. If the network is busy, it must wait for the conversation to end. A clear network prompts the node to try again at transmitting its message.

If two nodes happen to time out at the same time, another collision will occur. Ethernet solves this problem by aborting the network one more time and plugging new values into the timer equation. The new numbers are derived from certain parameters that are peculiar to one node only. In the unlikely event that another collision happens, the timer is incremented again with new numbers for another try. Each collision forces the node to wait longer before repeating the procedure. Multiple collisions are most likely to occur when several stations are vying for the network at the same time. After 16 unsuccessful attempts at avoiding a collision, the Ethernet node ceases trying and awaits further instructions.

If the collisions are due to a defect in the network, such as a streaming node or a cable problem, Ethernet activates a self-diagnostic program which can pinpoint the problem in moments and give you a reading.

WHO MANAGES THE NETWORK?

NETWORK MIXOLOGY

Altogether we have identified three network topologies and their variations: the star, the ring, and the bus. We have also examined three management schemes with their variations: centralized control, time slotted (including token passing), and contention. It is important to observe that any control strategy can be used with any topology.

10

HOW IS THE DATA SENT?

When a computer talks, it does so using digital pulses. These electrical pulses are binary coded with a voltage to represent numbers that are intelligible to the computer. The presence of a voltage indicates a 1, while its absence represents a 0. These binary *bits* represent quantities, much like the ABCs of our alphabet, and they can be organized into words called *bytes*. Explaining how these bits and bytes are used to communicate thoughts is the purpose of this chapter.

The word byte is made up of several bits arranged in a pattern. Most bytes contain eight bits. The expression 10101100, for instance, is a binary word that has a specific meaning, just as the word *table* has a meaning to us. While we identify with the word table, the computer relates to the word 10101100.

The sequence of the binary symbols is as important to the computer as are the alphabetical letters to us. If we take the word table and rearrange the letters to read bleat, it takes on an altogether different meaning. Likewise, the order of the 1s and 0s in a binary byte defines its meaning. The object of a local area network is to transport the binary word intact, without misplacing or losing any of its bits.

PARALLEL COMMUNICATIONS

A very simple way to do this is to provide a separate pathway for each bit to travel. Since most bytes are eight bits wide, we can compare our network to an eight-lane highway. Each bit travels in its own lane, and no one is allowed to cross into another lane for any reason. In that way, the word arrives at its destination in the same order in which it is transmitted.

To do this electronically, we replace the roadway with eight lengths of wire bundled into a cable. Each wire in the cable represents one lane of highway—and a certain position in the word. To send a byte across the network, the individual bits are placed on the cable in their respective positions and transmitted to the receiving node. This is called *parallel* communications because all bits are sent side by side in parallel order at the same time.

This approach is used extensively in computer communications, but it is generally limited to the very local level, such as inside the computer itself. It does, though, wander once in a while to the immediate outside of the machine. Your printer, for example, is probably connected to the computer through a multiwire cable using parallel interfacing. Other places you are likely to find parallel buses are in disk drives, monitors, and file servers.

The IEEE 488 bus, used by Hewlett-Packard and Commodore, is a parallel local area network that lies just on the borderline between a computer bus and a local area network. Initially designed by Hewlett-Packard to be an electronic instrument interface, the IEEE 488 has found acceptance in the networking community. It is used extensively to interconnect computers and peripherals, as well as instruments.

Unfortunately, parallel communications suffers from many shortcomings. In addition to requiring a separate wire for each data bit, most parallel networks also require handshaking signals that coordinate the transfer of data across the network. In the IEEE 488 bus, alone, there are no less than 13 individual wires. Not only does this make the cable expensive, but the sheer bulk of the cable makes it difficult to manage physically, a limitation that often locks the network into a distribution pattern that is not always easy to change. Each peripheral must tie into all network wires, and modifications to the network (the addition or deletion of equipment) is a major undertaking.

Its greatest drawback, however, is the potential for error, which increases as the length of the parallel bus increases—even when noise shielding techniques are employed.

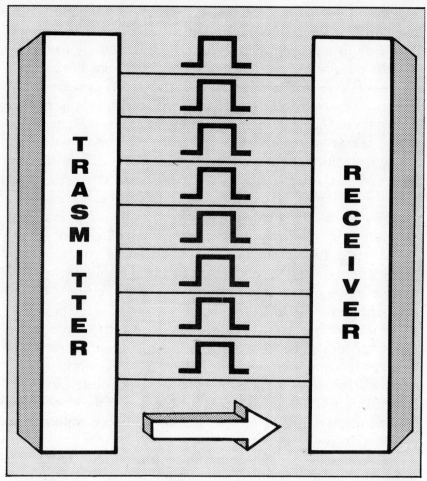

When computers talk, they do so using binary bits organized into words called bytes. The order of the bits in a binary word defines its meaning, just as the letters of our alphabet are arranged to spell words. The object of a local area network is to transport these words without losing the order. A very simple way to commun-icate digital information is to send it in parallel form. All bits are transmitted in unison and they all arrive at their destination at the same time and in the same order as they left. Parallel communications is generally limited to very local level, such as the data bus inside the computer itself.

SERIAL COMMUNICATIONS

To avoid these problems completely, the parallel communications bus is better replaced with a serial bus when sending data over distances greater than 10 feet. In serial communications, the data bits are extracted from the byte and sent out sequentially, one after the other instead of all at once. Morse code is a form of serial communications, with its continuous stream of dots and dashes. Serial communications is most often used in local area networks.

Serial communications transmits words sequentially, one letter at a time. Morse code is a form of serial communications with its continuous stream of dots and dashes. The speed at which the data is transmitted is called the baud rate. The higher the baud number, the faster the data flows. While serial communications is much slower than parallel, the error rate is considerably less and it is the preferred choice for LANs.

While serial communications is much slower because it takes eight times as long to send a byte, the error rate is considerably less. And that in itself more than makes up for the method's sluggishness. Furthermore, serial data will carry for longer distances before needing reamplification. Consequently, it is the preferred choice for LANs.

However, serial communications does present us with a problem. In parallel buses the bytes arrive at the receiving node in one piece, and it is clear by the rising edge of the incoming pulses when a byte has arrived. To read the word, the receiver simply scans the data field and notes which bits are present and which are missing.

But in serial communications, the bits arrive one at a time. This is fine so long as each bit is a 1, but the first time a 0 appears on the line it will go unnoticed. Why? Because the 0 is represented by a no-voltage state, a condition that also exists between data transmissions. How is the receiver to distinguish between the two?

To synchronize the transmitted data with the received data stream, a clock signal is generated along with the data. The clock pulses coincide exactly with the data bits and are sent over a separate line. Unlike the data stream, though, the clock has no missing pulses. Even when a 0 is broadcast on the data line, an accompanying pulse is sent over the clock line.

The receiver compares the clock pulses to the data stream. A coincidence of a clock pulse and a data bit means a 1 is present. If, however, a clock pulse arrives with no data pulse, the receiver interprets it as a 0. This form of synchronization is called *synchronous communications,* and it requires a master clock that feeds both the transmitter and receiver in order to work.

ASYNCHRONOUS COMMUNICATIONS

Another common form of data transmission that eliminates the need for a synchronizing master clock is *asynchronous communications.* Asynchronous serial communications relies on the fact that two clocks of approximately the same frequency will stay fairly well synchronized over a relatively short period of time.

HOW IS THE DATA SENT?

To synchronize the clocks initially, the transmitter sends out a timing signal called a *start bit*. The start bit forces the clock in the receiver to start in step with the transmitter. Following the start bit is the data byte. The receiver compares the incoming data to its internal clock to decide if the bit is a 1 or a 0, just as it does in synchronous communications. This time, however, the clock pulses are generated locally inside the receiver. It is normal for the receiver clock to drift a little during this sequence, but the change is not usually great enough to affect the proper capture of the short 8-bit stream.

At the end of it all is a *stop bit*. The stop bit is a unique clock pulse in that it is one-and-one-half clock periods wide, thus making it very distinguishable from the data bits. The receiver often uses this stop bit to determine if its clock has wandered too far askew during the transmission. If it has, a bit misalignment is declared and the word is discarded.

MANCHESTER ENCODING

Neither method, however, is entirely feasible all of the time. In many networks it is either impractical or too costly to install a master clock or include start and stop bits every few steps. To overcome this limitation, several encoding schemes have been devised in which synchronizing information is included right along with the data. *Manchester* encoding is by far the most popular.

The Manchester code, or biphase-L as it is technically known, is a self-clocking scheme that supplies synchronizing information right in the data stream. In Manchester code, clock and data pulses are combined so that each data bit is represented by a *transition* from high-to-low or low-to-high instead of being an actual voltage. The transitions occur in the *middle* of the bit rather than at its boundaries. The way they work it out, though, is a bit tricky.

With Manchester code, a 1 is represented by a low-to-high voltage transition. It doesn't matter what the actual voltage is; it is the swing from low to high that is important. A 0 is displayed by a swing from high to low. Here comes the tricky part. If there are more than two consecutive 1s or 0s in the data stream, the Manchester code adjusts for this so that the clocking part of the scheme remains intact.

When two 1s or two 0s occur in sequence, an intervening clock transition is inserted at the boundary—opposite that of the actual code—to correct the polarity of the line for the next voltage excursion. In other words, a clocking transition occurs at the real bit boundary when two or more consecutive figures occur. This guarantees that each cell bit contains information as to the value of the data bit. The clock monitors these changes for its synchronization.

BAUD RATES

The speed at which the data is transmitted is called the *baud* rate. Baud is measured in bits per second. A data rate of 300 bits per second, for instance, equals 300 baud. Likewise, 1200 bits per second translates into 1200 baud. The higher the baud number, the faster the data flows.

Baud rates can also give you an indication of approximately how

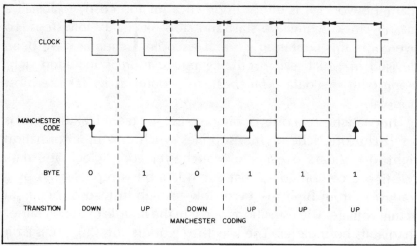

Decoding serial data is a little more difficult than parallel data because the presence of a clock pulse is required. The Manchester code is a self-clocking encoding scheme that supplies clocking information right in the data stream. In Manchester code, the data is represented by the transition of the voltage.

A 1 is represented by a low-to-high voltage swing, while 0s are displayed by a high-to-low transition sequence; an intervening clock transition is inserted at the bit boundary opposite that of the actual code to correct the polarity of the line for the next data bit.

many words per minute you are transmitting. As a rule of thumb, there is a direct correlation between bits per second and words per minute. A baud rate of 300 roughly means 300 words per minute; 1200 baud is 1200 words per minute.

Baud rates vary widely, depending upon the application and the equipment involved. Some of the more common speeds are 110, 300, 1200, 2400, 4800, 9600, and 19,600 baud. Of course, there are a host of others, climbing all the way into the megabaud range.

MESSAGE FRAMING

To make better use of the network, the data byte is often placed in a package called a frame. Frames are rigidly defined structures that hold networking instructions in addition to the actual word. One of the more popular data packets is Synchronous Data-Link Control (SDLC), first introduced by IBM.

In SDLC protocol, each frame begins with a sequence of bits called a *flag*. The flag is a unique binary pattern (01111110) that marks the boundaries of the packet. Each packet has an opening flag and a closing flag.

The opening flag is followed by an *address field*. The address field contains the address of the station for which the message is intended. When a listening node detects a flag pattern, it immediately compares the address field to its own identification address. If the addresses coincide, the node processes the frame. If they don't match, the node ignores the frame and goes back to looking for flags.

A *control field* follows the address field and contains command and response information essential to controlling the data link. This field also contains the number of frames that were used to transmit the whole message, plus the number of the current frame. The frames are numbered in consecutive order so the receiver will know if a frame is missing or received out of sequence.

Next in line is the *information field*, or I-field, as it is often abbreviated. This field contains the actual data byte. With SDLC protocol, this byte can be anywhere from one to eight bits long, depending upon the initial programming. Once established, the byte size can't be changed until new orders are issued.

After the data word is sent, the transmitter does a calculation using the data byte and first two fields (excluding the flag) as factors. The result of this algorithm (calculation) is a 16-bit number that is appended to the frame. This field is called a *field check sequence*. The receiver puts the received packet through the same mathematical equation and compares its answer to the number in the frame check sequence. If they match, the node is assured that the message arrived intact.

Finally, the frame is closed with another flag sequence. When more than one frame is sent, however, the flags butt up against each other and two flags will appear in a row—one ending and one beginning. To save time, the ending flag is normally dropped and the receiver recognizes the remaining one flag as both an ending and a beginning sequence.

But sending one word at a time over a LAN is not taking full advantage of the network. Conventional data-link protocols, such as SDLC and HDLC, were originally intended for wide area network use, such as telephone lines where bandwidth is limited and noise a problem. Consequently, they encourage the use of abbreviated addresses and single word packets. For similar reasons, wide area networks can neither provide for user identification nor support broadcast capabilities.

Obviously, this is not altogether satisfactory for local area networks. High performance demands higher-level protocols, which LANs are able to support. This is due in part to the fact that errors are less frequent and partly because there is no need to conserve bandwidth; LAN bandwidth is cheap and plentiful. Therefore, the data packets can be expanded to provide high-level control information and include more than one data byte.

ETHERNET PROTOCOL

Ethernet is a perfect example of what can be acheived by exploiting the full potential of a LAN. An Ethernet frame contains a preamble, two address fields, a type field, the data field, and a frame check sequence, in that order.

The Manchester-encoded *preamble* is an opening statement that synchronizes the receiver's clock to the transmitter, and generally lets everybody know a message is on its way. The preamble is a 64-bit word consisting of 62 alternating 1s and 0s, followed by a 11 ending (10101...01011).

The first of the two address fields is a 6-byte number representing one of three possible address destinations. It can be the address of an individual node for which the message is intended, or the address of a group of stations. Ethernet also contains a special code that allows a node to broadcast an announcement to every station on the network.

The second address field contains the address of the originating node. The *type field* is a 2-byte directive used to identify the user protocol associated with the frame.

The *data field* contains the actual message. A message, however, is not usually a fixed quantity; it may consist of any number of words. Therefore, the length of the data field is not fixed and may be adjusted to accommodate the information involved. However, the data field must not be shorter than 46 bytes or longer than 1500 bytes.

To ensure data fidelity, all fields (excluding the preamble) are subjected to processing by an error-detecting algorithm. The result of this calculation is entered into the *frame check sequence.*

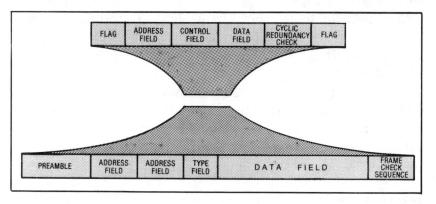

To make better use of the network, the data is placed in a package called a frame. Frames are rigidly defined structures that contain networking instructions in addition to the actual data. Along with the address of the intended receiver, every frame includes an error-checking algorithm. SDLC, HDLC, and X.25 (upper) are bit-oriented protocols that transmit only one word per frame. But sending one word at a time is not taking full advantage of the network. Ethernet (lower), a high-level protocol that can handle up to 1500 words per frame, is a perfect example of what can be achieved by exploiting the full potential of a LAN.

In analyzing the frame, the receiver performs the same calculation and compares its answer to the field sequence check. If they match, the data is considered valid.

As you can see, the throughput of data using a high-level protocol is much greater than for a bit-oriented packet. But it is not without its price. High-level protocols, like Ethernet, require substantially more software to work, software that must be contained either in the computer or in dedicated controller chips.

BASEBAND NETWORKS

Local area networks, as a whole, fall into two distinct categories, baseband and broadband. Most networks are of the *baseband* design. In a baseband network, the digital pulses are placed directly onto the network wires. No elaborate schemes are used; either the voltage is there or it isn't. The receiver gauges these voltage levels and uses them to reconstruct the original message.

You might best compare a baseband network to a stereo system. When you connect your stereo to a speaker through a pair of wires, the signal travels down the wires at its original frequency to the speaker. The speaker then takes this voltage and translates it into air pressure that we perceive as sound. Likewise, a baseband network takes the digital pulses and places them on the network in raw form. The node then processes the voltages and changes them back into data.

Theoretically, baseband networks have unlimited bandwidth, which means data throughput is unlimited. The only limiting factor is the frequency response of the network medium. Coaxial cable can accommodate band widths up to 300 MHz, while fiber optics easily stretches that figure twentyfold.

BROADBAND NETWORKS

The second method by which local networks convey information is the *broadband* network. In broadband, the digital pulses are not placed directly on the network. Instead, they modulate a carrier frequency that transports the information. For the sake of argument, let's compare the broadband network to a TV set.

With television you have the option of selecting from several channels at the twist of a knob. This is made possible through frequency allocation. The radio spectrum, which includes television, is made up of a whole range of different frequencies. A television set has the ability to zero in on one particular frequency and monitor its activity. When it does, we see it as a television channel.

This is achieved by a technique called *frequency multiplexing*. That is where several different channels are stacked one atop another by assignment of a base frequency called a *carrier*. The carrier is a radio frequency many times greater than the frequency of the signal we wish to pass through the channel, and each channel has its own specific carrier frequency which is different from all the other channels. We choose the one we wish to watch by scanning the radio spectrum with the channel changer.

In a similar fashion, LAN networks are often divided into frequency slots. Each division is an entire network in itself, as TV channels are individual to themselves. This means that you can have five or six (or more) networks operating through a single cable, the way television signals travel through CATV systems.

To permit talk on a channel, the carrier is modulated. Many modulating techniques are in common use, some of them probably already familiar to you. There are amplitude modulation (AM),

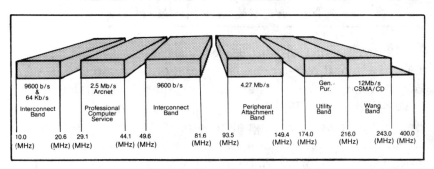

9600 b/s & 64 Kb/s	2.5 Mb/s Arcnet	9600 b/s	4.27 Mb/s	Gen. Pur.	12Mb/s CSMA/CD
Interconnect Band	Professional Computer Service	Interconnect Band	Peripheral Attachment Band	Utility Band	Wang Band

10.0 (MHz)	20.6 (MHz)	29.1 (MHz)	44.1 (MHz)	49.6 (MHz)	81.6 (MHz)	93.5 (MHz)	149.4 (MHz)	174.0 (MHz)	216.0 (MHz)	243.0 (MHz)	400.0 (MHz)

Local area networks, as a whole, fall into two categories: baseband networks and broadband networks. Baseband networks place the digital pulses directly on the network, while broadband uses a modulated carrier frequency to convey information, much in the same way that radio waves carry information through the air. The network is divided into radio channels similar to the channels of a television set. Each channel is a network in itself. WangNet, for instance, has eleven local area networks operating through the same cable.

frequency modulation (FM), frequency-shifted keying (FSK), and many others. With television, the carrier is modulated with picture and sound information. In a broadband LAN, the carrier is modulated by digital pulses.

In most broadband networks, channels are assigned specific duties. Let's take WangNet, for example, one of the more popular broadband networks. Wang uses a 390-MHz-wide communications band extending from 10 MHz to 400 MHz for its network. The network is divided into six frequency slots.

Each slot, or segment, is a LAN channel, and each channel has a particular function to perform. The utility band, for instance, is reserved for video communications, such as teleconferencing. The Wang band serves Wang business computers. The newest band to be exploited is the Professional Computer Service band. It uses a 15-MHz segment of the 390-MHz WangNet frequency spectrum, beginning at 29 MHz and extending to 44 MHz. Within this band are five individual channels, each 3 MHz wide, that Wang has designated as personal computer communication channels. Each channel can be used for a local area network capable of supporting up to 255 nodes. As demand increases, it is likely that Wang will open up additional channels, thus expanding its network with no modification to the original cable installation.

NETWORK TURNAROUND

Although a broadband network can support more than one LAN at a time through channel separation, it doesn't come without problems. The most significant problem is *crosstalk*.

When piping radio frequencies through a coaxial cable, it is desirable to have all the signals flowing in the same direction. This means that it is not advisable to mix the signals by giving the nodes unrestricted use of the network medium. If you take a length of coax and inject a signal into each open end, a predictable thing happens. Where the two signals meet, an interference pattern is set up, not unlike the merging ripples you see when two stones are cast into a pond of water. The result is signal distortion.

If, however, the waves are traveling all the same direction, they have no opportunity to mix and distort. This can be demonstrated by throwing two stones into the same pond at exactly the same spot. The two sets of ripples still travel outward from each rock, but now they don't override each other.

Broadband networks avoid the crosstalk problem by forcing data to flow unidirectionally through the coax by dividing the node into distinct transmit and receive ports. Through the transmit port it is possible to talk, but not to listen. Likewise, the receiver port has ears, but no voice.

Broadband networks achieve this division in two different ways. WangNet uses two separate cables for its LAN. One is outgoing, the other is incoming. The way it is done, though, is somewhat unique. In actuality, there is only one cable. What Wang has done is connect all the transmitting ports to a single cable using conventional unidirectional cable splitters. All nodes feed the same cable. After the coax has snaked its way through all stations, it takes a U-turn and doubles back on itself. It then begins the process of attaching itself to the receiver ports in reverse order for the return trip.

There is only one way for a transmitted signal to travel: from the beginning of the network to the end. Therefore, no mixing of the signals can occur, hence no crosstalk. The node sees two cables; the network supports only one.

Another common technique which eliminates the hassle of having to install dual coaxial cables and permits the use of a single line is to divide the transmit and receive functions into two widely separated frequency bands. Let's examine LocalNet 20, by Sytek. It is such a network.

LocalNet 20 uses two 36-MHz bandwidths for its transmit and receive functions. The frequencies from 70 MHz to 106 MHz are used to transmit information. All nodes feed the coax at these frequencies when talking, and all data on all channels flows in one direction through the cable.

At the *head end* of the cable is a frequency converter. It takes the incoming transmitted frequencies and converts them into higher frequencies. The new frequencies occupy the 226-MHz to

262-MHz portion of the radio spectrum. This new 36-MHz-wide band is retransmitted over the network cable in the *opposite* direction.

The receivers in the LAN are tuned to this band, and all nodes intercept their messages on these frequencies. Consequently, a memo sent by you on the 70-MHz channel is converted and returned to you at 226 MHz. These two frequencies are spaced far enough apart that the little bit of interference they generate is not significant enough to disturb the network.

The initial cost of a broadband network compared to a baseband network, though, is considerably greater. The entire system must be purchased and installed at one time, there is no a-little-here, a-little-there way of putting things together. Expanding the system, however, is an altogether different matter. Since all the hardware already exists, adding another channel to a broadband network is relatively inexpensive, whereas expanding a baseband network is equivalent to installing a new network.

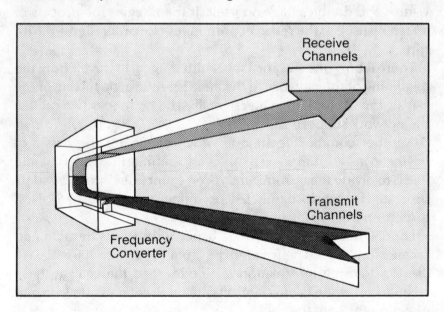

Broadband networks require dedicated transmit and receive ports for their operation. A single port can be used if a frequency converter is installed at the head end of the coax cable. The converter receives the transmitted signals, changes their carrier frequency to a higher range, and retransmits the new signal back over the network. The receivers in the LAN are tuned to this new band, and all nodes intercept their messages at the higher frequency.

11

WHAT IF THERE IS AN ERROR?

Whenever data is moved from one place to another, there is always the possibility for error. Errors can creep into the network in many different ways. Collisions, network noise, external noise, framing errors, and misplaced data bits all take their toll. A single component failure within a node, or a noise spike on any one of the network links, can easily change a 0 into a 1, or vice versa.

And since digital codes depend upon 100-percent accuracy, one misaligned bit could change the true meaning of a message. As a result, an entire branch of computer science has developed around the detection and correction of data transmission errors. This technology is divided into two groups of error handling: methods that detect errors and those which correct errors. Of course, the first thing that must be done in either case is to devise some way of detecting an error before it has become a permanent part of the message.

ERROR DETECTION

The simpler methods are sometimes the best. Rings and loops, for instance, have their own special brand of error checking which involves little work. As you're aware, messages sent over the ring are handled by each succesive node until they finally reach their destination. This type of information handling invites errors.

Once the data has reached its goal, though, the receiving station has two options, both of which are conducive to error detection. The node may regenerate the message or remove it. If the node chooses the former option, it reconstructs the message and continues passing it around the ring, just as if the data was intended for another station. Finally, the data ends up where it began, at the originating node. The originating node now reviews the data stream and compares it to the original message. If it has arrived intact, the node assumes it was received and processed properly.

In the latter case, the receiving node is required to remove the message and replace it with an acknowledgment. A negative acknowledgment means the message was either not properly received or not understood. Unfortunately, neither method assures completely error-free transmission. Even if the originating station agrees that the data was returned unchanged, there is no guarantee that a malfunction inside the receiver itself—which is actually separate from the reconstruction circuitry—didn't mishandle or interpret the data differently.

PARITY

To resolve the problem, an error-detecting code must be sent along with the data byte, a code that remains with it at all times. This code contains information that allows the receiver to make a decision about the fidelity of the digital data. A very common form of error detecting is byte *parity*.

Byte parity works very simply. It exploits the fact that every byte has either an odd or an even number of 1s in its spelling. Let's take the word 10101010 as an example. It has an even number of ones in its data—four, to be exact. By changing the last digit from a 0 to a 1, though, we change the parity of the byte. The new word, 10101011, has an odd parity because it contains five 1s, an odd number.

To use this fact for error detection, the transmitter counts the number of 1s in the byte and attaches a parity bit to the word. This ninth bit, which is permanently appended to the data byte and transmitted right along with the actual data, guarantees that the parity of the byte will always be odd. If the word contains an even

WHAT HAPPENS IF THERE IS AN ERROR?

number of 1s, the transmitter adds an extra 1 to the ninth position so that the count changes to odd. If the byte is already odd, a 0 is inserted into the ninth spot.

When the data byte and its parity bit arrive at the destination, the receiver counts the number of 1s in the packet. If it comes out odd, then the word was received as transmitted. If, on the other hand, the number of 1s happens to be even, the receiver immediately identifies that word as being in error and sets a parity flag. Errors can occur through the loss of a data bit or the misinterpretation of a data bit.

Actually, there are two types of parity check: odd parity, which we have just examined, and even parity. Even parity, the counterpart of odd, defines its bytes by an even number of 1s. Odd parity, however, is the more versatile of the two and the preferred choice.

In odd parity, the word 00000000 becomes 000000001. A byte with all 0s in it, including the parity bit, is an error condition in odd-parity parlance. With even parity the word becomes 000000000, a sequence which could go undetected in some coding schemes.

Parity is the cornerstone of most error-detecting schemes. Parity exploits the fact that all digital words have either an odd or even number of 1s in their spelling, that relationship being dependent upon the actual organization of the data bits. The technique uses an extra parity bit to change the odd/even value of the word. If the word contains an even number of 1s, and you wish to express odd parity, the parity bit is made a 1. In the final count, now, there are an odd number of 1s in the sequence. If the word already contains an odd number of 1s, a 0 is entered into the parity bit. To check for transmitted errors, the total number of 1s in the word and parity bit are counted. An even count indicates that one of the bits was received in error.

Parity checking does have its shortcomings, though. In most networks, the extra bit added to each word for parity error detection is too wasteful to be desirable. The addition of an extra bit for every word means a 12.5-percent loss in data throughput.

The situation is further aggravated by the fact that parity is a *single-error* detection scheme—which means that if one bit in a byte changes, an error will be announced. If *two* errors occur, however, the number count will switch back to odd due to the introduction of the second failed bit. As a result, the receiver will accept the phony word as valid and include it in the data stream, where it will undoubtedly cause problems later down the line.

The probability of several errors occurring as a group is greater than that of random errors. This is due in large part to the nature of noise, which has a tendency to occur in bursts rather than periodically.

CHECKSUM

Consequently, a checksum method, called *cyclic redundancy checking* (CRC), was developed. CRC checksum error detection spots errors within the entire data packet rather than in the individual bytes that make up the packet. This is accomplished by taking all the bytes in the frame and adding them together. The result of this operation is placed within a special *frame check sequence* that is appended to the message, as was revealed in Chapter 10.

After receiving a data packet, the receiver puts the data bytes through the same mathematical process and compares its answer to the sum arrived at by the transmitter. The logic behind this scheme is that if any of the bytes changed in value during their journey, the sums will differ. Granted, there is no way of determining in which byte the error occurred, but it doesn't really matter. The entire frame is simply discarded and a new one requested.

POLYNOMIC CHECKSUMS

Instead of simple arithmetic being used to arrive at the checksum answer, though, a complex polynomial equation is often chosen. This algorithm is designed to provide the most accurate way of checking for errors without introducing errors of its own. The checksum sequence for an Ethernet packet, for instance, is : $x^{32} + x^{26} + x^{23} + x^{22} + x^{16} + x^{12} + x^{11} + x^{10} + x^8 + x^7 + x^5 + x^4 + x^2 + x + 1 = G(x)$, where $G(x)$ is the checksum total. The results of this extensive calculation are placed in the 32-bit frame check sequence.

As you may have guessed by now, the checksum total is considerably longer than the space provided for it in the frame check sequence. This is the case with most error-detecting schemes. If we tried to include the entire figure in the frame, it would be larger than the information portion of the packet itself. The solution is to simply let the sum overflow the CRC byte with no regard to the overflow pattern. Only the least significant bytes are saved, and these are sufficient to indicate an error.

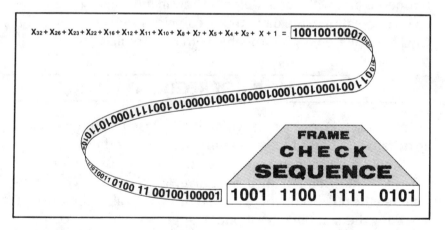

Cyclic redundancy checking (CRC) error detection spots errors within an entire data frame rather than in the individual bytes that make up the packet. This is done by subjecting the data bits to a complex algorithm and putting the answer in the frame check sequence of the data packet. The equation above is the CRC algorithm for Ethernet protocol. Because the frame check sequence is only 32 bits long and the algorithm answer much longer, the answer is allowed to overflow the frame with only the least significant bits being saved. The receiver checks for errors by grinding the data through the same algorithm and comparing answers. A difference in solutions means a mistake occurred. Granted there is no way to determine which byte is in error, but it really doesn't matter. Data recovery is done through retransmission.

Before the checksum number is placed into the CRC frame, though, it is usually complemented (inverted) by a change in the polarity of the bits: 1s become 0s and 0s turn into 1s.

At the receiving node, the data frame is processed—CRC field and all. The result of this processing produces an answer that is always consistent in value—no matter what actual numbers were used to design the frame check sequence—if the frame is valid. With Ethernet, the algorithm for a valid frame always equals 11000111 00000100 11011101 01111011. Any other answer indicates an error.

Notice that the larger the frame becomes, the more efficiently the CRC is used. In an Ethernet frame, for instance, it occupies a scant 0.25 percent of the packet. One common misconception about parity and checksums, in general, is that the extra bits of code added to the byte or frame must be transmitted accurately to perform the error-checking task. This is not true. All bits are treated identically, and an error in the transmission of a check bit will be discovered as quickly as an error in the data package. Erroneous data will pass undetected only in the unlikely event that an error created in the data stream coincides with an error in the CRC field (extremely improbable with polynomials).

ERROR CORRECTION

But, in fact, errors are unavoidable. In practice, the detected error rate is reported to be one in a billion. In other words, for every billion bits of data you transmit, one will arrive in error.

To put that number in perspective, let's say that you were assigned the task of copying a list of figures. Let's also suppose that you copy them at the rate of one digit per second and you keep this up day and night, 24 hours a day without stopping. At this rate, it will be 31 years before you commit your first mistake! And unless you began at a very early age, you probably won't live long enough to commit a second.

That's how small one in a billion is. In the normal scheme of things, it is infinitesimal. But in a network operating at the relatively slow speed of 10 MHz, you can expect an error every 1.6 minutes. That is not infinitesimal.

WHAT HAPPENS IF THERE IS AN ERROR?

One or two errors might not be critical in a message consisting only of words. Such errors most likely result in typos that are easily identified and corrected. But for transactions containing numeric data, an error that changes a figure or moves a decimal point would probably go unnoticed. And for many applications, such as bank transactions, such errors are intolerable. Therefore, it is important that an error be spotted and corrected as soon as possible.

When an error occurs, a new data packet is normally requested to replace the defective one. In some situations, however, it is either not possible or not desirable to retransmit data. Fortunately, the need for retransmitting data can be totally eliminated by using error-correcting codes.

Error-correcting codes use mathematical techniques to identify and correct errors. A common error-correcting code is the *Hamming code*. This coding scheme relies on parity bits that are intermixed with the data bits in the byte. Combining the parity and data bits according to a strict set of parity equations makes it possible to pinpoint accurately the location and nature of the error.

Basically, error correction is accomplished by redefining the binary values of a number. The number 7, for instance, would normally be expressed as 0111 in binary language. In Hamming code, it is 0001111. The first two bits and the fourth bit are parity checks.

By plugging the Hamming-coded word into the equations, you not only can tell if any bit is changed in value, but you can also locate its position in the word. For example, if the number 7 is accidentally transmitted as 0011111, the Hamming code equations inform you first that there is an error because no such code word exists. The algorithms then go on to tell you that the mistake is in the third bit. Armed with this information, you make a simple change in the third bit, from 1 to 0, to correct the word to its proper value, the number 7.

Unlike simple parity, the Hamming code (and others like it) can detect errors of two or more bits, though it can only correct single bit errors. The overhead required to generate and check error-correcting Hamming codes, however, is quite complex. Each byte requires the calculation of no less than six equations.

Value	Position						
	1	2	3	4	5	6	7
	p_1	p_2	m_1	p_3	m_2	m_3	m_4
0	0	0	0	0	0	0	0
1	1	1	0	1	0	0	1
2	0	1	0	1	0	1	0
3	1	0	0	0	0	1	1
4	1	0	0	1	1	0	0
5	0	1	0	0	1	0	1
6	1	1	0	0	1	1	0
7	0	0	0	1	1	1	1
8	1	1	1	0	0	0	0
9	0	0	1	1	0	0	1

m = data bit
p = parity bit

Value = m_4, m_3, m_2, m_1 (binary)
(5 = 0101 for example)

$p_1 = \overline{m_1 + m_2 + m_4}$

$p_2 = \overline{m_1 + m_3 + m_4}$

$p_3 = \overline{m_2 + m_3 + m_4}$

$C_3 = p_1 + m_1 + m_2 + m_4$

$C_2 = p_2 + m_1 + m_3 + m_4$

$C_1 = p_3 + m_2 + m_3 + m_4$

C_1, C_2, C_3 binary = binary value pointing to *position* of error.

	1	2	3	4	5	6	7
Good value 7 =	0	0	0	1	1	1	1
Transmission error value =	0	0	1	1	1	1	1

Using above equations: $C_1 = 0$ $C_2 = 1$ $C_3 = 1$
Error position = 011 = position 3.
Changing position 3 from 1 to 0 yields:
$\qquad$ 0001111, the corrected value.

A common error-correcting code is the Hamming code. This coding scheme relies on parity bits that are interspersed among the data bits. The positions of the parity bits are rigidly defined and their value is calculated by the above equations. To correct for an error, the data and the parity bits are run through the bottom three equations. The relative value of the three answers points to the defective bit. In the example above, a simple value change in the third bit recovers the erroneous data to the original number 7.

BLOCK CODES

Another approach to error correcting is arranging the bytes in a two-dimensional matrix. This technique is called block coding. Suppose you wanted to send three bytes of data, such as 10110010 01110100 01110100. If the digits were written into a four-by-six matrix, they would look like this:

1	0	1	1	0	0
1	0	0	1	1	1
0	1	0	0	0	1
1	1	0	1	0	0

Now to each row and column of this matrix is added a check digit that brings the parity of each row and column to an even number of 1s. In the first column, there are three 1s, so a parity 1 is added, making the total four, an even number. The second column has two 1s, already an even number, so a 0 parity digit is added to that column. The same is done for the remaining columns and all four rows. The resulting grid looks like this:

	1	0	1	1	1	0
1	1	0	1	1	0	0
0	1	0	0	1	1	1
0	0	1	0	0	0	1
1	1	1	0	1	0	0

All the digits are then transmitted, left to right and top to bottom, to form the word 101110110110001001110010011110100.

The receiver recreates the matrix and places the digits into their respective squares. It then checks for errors by comparing parity. Let's suppose an error occurred in the third column of the first row like this:

	1	0	1	1	1	0
1	1	0	0	1	0	0
0	1	0	0	1	1	1
0	0	1	0	0	0	1
1	1	1	0	1	0	0

Notice that both the third column and the first row of the matrix now have an odd parity. The receiver notes this and declares an error. To recover from the mistake, the receiver changes the bit defect at the point where the defective columns and rows intersect, thereby restoring the matrix to its original form:

	1	0	1	1	1	0
1	1	0	1	1	0	0
0	1	0	0	1	1	1
0	0	1	0	0	0	1
1	1	1	0	1	0	0

WHAT HAPPENS IF THERE IS AN ERROR?

This simple code can also correct errors that occur in one of the parity bits. Let's say the check bit for the fourth column is received as follows:

	1	0	1	0	1	0
1	1	0	1	1	0	0
0	1	0	0	1	1	1
0	0	1	0	0	0	1
1	1	1	0	1	0	0

In this situation, only the fourth column has odd parity. All the rows still retain even parity. This arrangement tells the receiver that the error is in the parity check bit and not in the message; therefore, no further action is needed.

Of course, this is only an elementary example. In actual practice, the algorithms are more complex and the ratio of parity bits to message bits is much larger. One of the more popular error-correcting block codes is the *Reed-Solomon code*.

With Reed-Solomon code, there is a list of acceptable code words in block form. When a message is received, it is checked against the list. If the block is not on the list because of incurred errors, the receiver must make a determination of its original context. It does this by statistically searching the files for words that are similar to the received word. It then compares these words and chooses the one in which the fewest changes have to be made.

The Reed-Solomon code has found extensive application in military communications for recovering data from enemy jamming attempts. The Reed-Solomon code is also extremely valuable in LAN applications because of the burst-like nature of network interference. Single errors are rare. Most errors tend to occur in bursts where many digits in a sequence are affected by the same noise source. The Reed-Solomon code, when properly installed, can correct for as many as 5000 damaged bits at a time.

CONVOLUTIONAL CODES

Competing with block codes are convolutional error-correcting codes, like the one developed by Andrew J. Viterbi, formerly of UCLA and now president of Linkabit, a communications corporation. Convolutional codes use an algorithm that By statistically comparing a received message to the probability of what the message originally said, corrections are made. The Viterbi convolution error-correcting code finds wide application in satellite networks.

	1	0	1	1	1	0
1	1	0	1	1	0	0
0	1	0	0	1	1	1
1	0	1	0	0	0	1
1	1	1	0	1	0	0

Two-dimensional matrix blocks are also used to detect and correct errors. In this method, the parity of each column and row is brought to an even count of 1s by the insertion of a parity digit check. The entire matrix is then transmitted over the LAN, check bits and all. At the receiver, the matrix is reconstructed and the message and check digits placed in their respective squares. An odd parity of either a column or a row indicates an error in the message. Errors are corrected by changing the value of the bit where the oddly numbered column and row intersect.

12

CAN I INTERFACE ONE NETWORK TO ANOTHER?

By their very definition, local area networks are geographically limited communications systems. And when our communications needs exceed the limits of the LAN, most of us feel that we are faced with the expensive dilemma of switching to a wide area network with its obvious speed and data transfer limitations.

Fortunately, there is an alternative called subnetworking. Essentially, subnetworking solves the problem by interconnecting two or more local area networks. You might want to compare this to a ring network with several nodes in its loop. Now imagine each node not as an individual station, but as a cluster of stations. Each cluster is a *subnetwork*. Subnetworks function much like individual departments in a large corporation. Each department is run by a supervisor who coordinates the communications needs within the department. From time to time, though, the department heads gather in a meeting to exchange data and ideas among themselves. Subnetworking lets networks talk among themselves.

This concept has many advantages. First, and foremost, the approach is modular and you can reduce your overall networking costs by adding small local area networks as the need arises, and connecting them together as they are installed. It also permits you to tailor the individual subnetworks to specific needs. Slower or less reliable networks, for example, may be installed in certain less critical applications to save money. And the consequence of one network failing does not have the same impact as it does on a single LAN because the failure is restricted to the area it serves.

Before I lead you into believing subnetworking to be a panacea, let me say it does have its limitations. The disadvantages of this arrangement are increased complexity and the possibility that some network functions, notably the low-level acknowledgments used in some rings, cannot operate across network boundaries. Overall, though, the advantages far outweigh the disadvantages.

BRIDGES

Networks are linked together through a device called a *bridge*. Basically, a bridge is a communications device that selectively passes data from one network to another. For the sake of this discussion, we must assume both networks to be identical. A difference in protocol between networks creates a language barrier with which a simple bridge is incapable of coping. More on that later.

Let's examine the workings of subnetworking by giving ourselves a scenario to walk through. Let's say you are a department supervisor of shipping and receiving in a large manufacturing firm. And because your product volume is so extensive, your company has leased a separate building for you and your crew to handle nothing but shipping and receiving.

Somewhere in the corporate offices is the accounting department, headed up by Mary. Now each of you has a local area network to serve your needs. Your network ties together the many machines needed by your staff, such as the dispatching computer, labeling machine, and so forth. Mary's LAN binds the many terminals used by the several accountants she employs for input to the mainframe computer at corporate headquarters.

Unfortunately, the distance separating the two facilities is great enough to prevent the two networks from being combined into one. Your problem, then, is to connect your network with Mary's so that you can feed her billing information and she can forward shipping orders to you.

The bridge is your link. The bridge would most naturally be located at a point where the two subnetworks are physically adjacent.

CAN I INTERFACE ONE NETWORK TO ANOTHER?

Inside the bridge are three essential components: an interface, a filter, and a buffer. Each element has a specific duty attached to it for the transfer of data across network lines. First is the *interface*.

Actually, the bridge contains two interface elements. One interface belongs to your side of the bridge, and one goes to Mary's side. The interface is a node-matching device that also supplies a fair amount of amplification to the signals so that voltage levels are compatible after their long journey.

The heart of the bridge, however, is the *filter*. It is the filter that decides which data packets are allowed to cross and which aren't. Let's say you wish to communicate with Bob, your trucking dispatcher. All you have to do is call him up on your computer and the network will do the rest. The filter recognizes this as an internal message and prevents it from crossing the bridge.

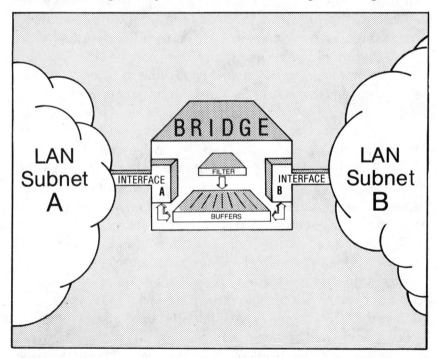

In many situations, it is either essential or more advantageous to connect two smaller LANs together than it is to use one larger LAN. When connecting similar networks, a device known as a bridge is used. The bridge is a communications device that selectively passes data from one network to another. The interface section of the bridge actually becomes an integral part of each network and behaves much like any other node. The data flows from network to network through the buffer under filter control.

A note to Mary, on the other hand, is handled differently. First, you must enter the address of Mary's department, since she is on another network, then her name. The filter recognizes the LAN address as a directive and passes the data packet through Mary's network, where it is routed to her desk.

This is where the *buffer* comes in. Various timing differences between the networks—even identical networks—demand that data first be stored in a buffer. The buffer is nothing more than a small memory bank that can hold up to several thousand bytes of information. The bridge accepts data from your network and tucks it away in the buffer until it can be transferred.

The bridge now looks for an opportunity to transmit on Mary's network, according to traffic load. For instance, if the network is in use when the data packet arrives at the buffer, the bridge must wait for a break in traffic before dumping the contents of the buffer into the network. In effect, the bridge has essentially become a participating node in Mary's network and it must follow network protocol and access rules.

During periods of heavy use, it is possible to overfill a buffer before it has an opportunity to transfer its message, in which case the bridge discards data packets according to previously pro-grammed procedure. This is an acceptable practice since most LAN protocols are generally prepared to handle lost packets. Recent experience with Ethernet operating between networks, though, shows that very few packets are ever discarded in reality.

Buffers can also be used to match speeds in networks with similar protocol but different data rates. This allows you to have an inexpensive, low-performance network with light duties inter-mesh with a high-speed, high-performance LAN

When transmitting data across networks, you must take into consideration the addressing of the data packet. Unless address-ing is very clear, your message could end up on the wrong net-work, or on more than one network. The effort to make network addressing precise has resulted in development of more than one scheme. Some schemes rely on hierarchical layering, others use extended address fields to hold a presumably larger address. We have just reviewed one called *source routing*. Filters that imple-ment source routing are extremely simple; indeed, that's what makes it the most popular for small LANS.

MODEMS: THE LONG – DISTANCE BRIDGE

There are situations in which it is not possible to bring two subnetworks physically close enough to be joined by an ordinary bridge. An example would be a university with a local area network on campus and a major research center across town. It is assumed that the distance involved is beyond the range of twisted pairs or coax cable. For circumstances such as these, the networks can be tied together by a long-distance bridge known as a *modem*.

You could actually define the modem as a half-bridge. Inside each modem are a filter, a buffer, and *one* interface. In fact, many modems don't even contain full buffering capabilities. They rely, instead, on the virtual memory of the host interface device. A modem is placed in each subnetwork and the two half-bridges are joined with a length of cable—a long distance-link.

Because of easy accessibility and low costs, the long-distance link is generally a leased telephone line. Modems communicate over the phone line using a *carrier frequency*. Although it would be easier to simply place the digital signal directly on the lines themselves, it is virtually impossible to pass digital pulses through the telephone network. It was never designed to accommodate them. It was designed, instead, for the human voice, which occupies the spectrum between 300 and 3500 Hz.

What the modem does is take the digital pulses and use them to modulate a carrier frequency that falls within this narrow audio range. Two modulation techniques are commonly used for modems. One is frequency modulation, the other is phase-shift modulation.

Frequency modulation begins by taking the digital pulse and encoding it into a frequency. One specific frequency is used to represent a logic 1, and a different frequency represents a logic 0. With binary coding, only two frequencies are needed. As the train of pulses enters the modem, the pulses are changed into their respective audio tones, the frequency of the tone corresponding to a logic state, and sent over the phone line in serial form. The characteristic output sound produces a "doo-dah" effect. This form of frequency modulation is called *frequency-shifted keying*

111

(FSK) because the frequencies shift back and forth according to the digital encoding.

At the receiving end of the conversation is the other modem bridge. The filter in the receiver converts the encoded frequencies back into digital pulses and places them in the buffer for distribution to the network.

Pulse modulation encodes the digital bits on the carrier by shifting the phase of the sine wave back and forth, thus earning it the name of *phase-shifted keying (PSK)*. Unlike FSK modulation, a constant carrier frequency is used with the relative phase of the carrier indicating the value of the binary bit. Because the relative phase of the carrier is important, and not its absolute value, most PSK schemes use differential phase encoding (DPSK). DPSK measures the phase of the carrier in two successive bits in order to determine the phase change. The actual shift occurs at a specific point on the sine wave, and not necessarily on the pulse boundaries.

With either modulation technique, bilateral communications is accomplished by placing each conversation on a separate audio channel. In this way, the two modems can be talking at the same time to each other over a single phone line. This is known as *full-duplex* communications. If only one modem is talking while the other listens, it is *half-duplex* (sometimes referred to as simplex).

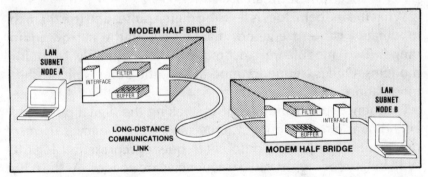

There are situations where it is not physically possible to bring the two networks close enough together to be joined by an ordinary bridge. In this event, the networks can be coupled with a long-distance link called a modem. Basically, a modem is a half-bridge, that connects to a network node. And because it is a half-bridge, one modem is required for each network. Easy accessibility and low cost generally leads to the use of leased telephone lines for the long-distance link.

CAN I INTERFACE ONE NETWORK TO ANOTHER?

Of course, it is possible—and sometimes mandatory—for the long-distance bridge communications link to be of lower bandwidth than the two subnetworks it interconnects. In fact, modems are generally very slow devices. The most common modem speed is 300 baud—or about 300 words per minute. All 300-baud modems adhere to Bell's 103 standard that stipulates FSK encoding. The next step up is the 1200-baud modem which transmits about 1200 words per minute and uses Bell 212A PSK encoding. Larger commercial modems come in speed increments of 2400, 4800, and 9600 baud. Recently, AT&T announced the release of leased telephone lines that will handle 56K-baud rates.

Due to the quality of telephone communications, though, the error rate is high, and the chances for errors increase as speed increases. Error detection is usually accomplished by having the receiving modem echo the data back over the reverse audio channel as it receives it—*echoplexing*, as this is commonly called.

Long-distance modem bridges can also be established using radio transmission or fiber optics. Where traffic is heavy, dedicated digital facilities may be installed, such as packet-switching services.

GATEWAYS

So far our discussion of network interfacing has assumed that all the networks are alike; that is, they all have identical protocols even though their needs may vary. But often the network user is faced with the problem of interconnecting dissimilar networks—networks that have no values in common.

The need to interconnect dissimilar local networks may arise in several different ways. There may be technical reasons for installing LANs with different facilities. The administrative offices of a university, for example, may require a sophisticated high-speed bus network to handle the huge flow of data passing among its departments. The university laboratory, on the other hand, requires a network with extremely low error rates, so their choice is a low-speed ring. By the nature of its functions, each network supports a different protocol.

113

Even when no adequate technical reason exists, there may still be network incompatibility within departments of a company. Although little need for intercommunication may be apparent at the time of installation, such needs have a habit of surfacing over time as the scope of the system grows and the ambitions of the developers increase. Finally, there is the question of cost. Even if an organization is willing and able to standardize on Ethernet or another proprietary product, it may be unable to justify the cost for all areas involved. The result is an odd assortment of networks distributed throughout the facility.

The problem encountered in internetworking dissimilar local area networks is the same problem faced by people of different nationalities. There is a language barrier. For instance, let's say that at a cocktail party we have four very distinguished guests who hail from four different countries: Japan, France, Germany, and Bri-

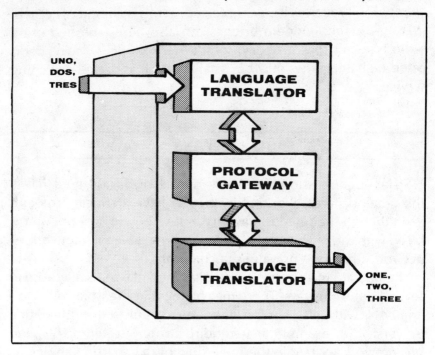

When interconnecting dissimilar networks, one frequently encounters a protocol language barrier. The words spoken by one network are usually quite foreign to the other. To solve the problem, the networks are bridged with an intelligent device called a gateway. Like a foreign language interpreter, the gateway translates between the two protocols. Emulators are excellent examples of protocol conversion.

tain. Each is very proficient in his native tongue but has no knowledge of other languages. The four try futilely to indulge in conversation.

An identical situation arises in the attempt to interconnect dissimilar networks. The words spoken by one are quite foreign to the other. To solve the problem, the subnetworks are bridged with an intelligent device called a *gateway*. Basically, the gateway is a protocol converter that translates between the languages, just as a language interpreter would have been a most welcome sight at our cocktail party. Gateways can take the form of a bridge or a modem.

The problems of protocol conversion, however, extend beyond the obvious. Put simply, there's more to it than the simple restating of words to make them understood. There are problems in restructuring addresses, error control, and flow control. Internetting a bus to a ring, for instance, usually involves changing the addressing procedure because one is a sequential network while the other is broadcast. Error detection techniques may also differ, and the gateway must be able to translate the procedures properly.

It has been suggested that the only plausible solution to internetting is to structure all protocols in hierarchical layers. In fact, the international committee of ISO is working toward this goal. Unfortunately, this approach itself poses some problems since older networks have not been designed on the basis of a layered model, and even where this has been done, differences of intention and interpretation are apparent. Clearly, messages cannot be transferred from sophisticated to simple systems without some loss of function.

Nevertheless, gateways do exist. At present, most of them are specially tailored items designed for the individual situation. Special interfaces of hardware and software must be designed into the gateway from inception, and the chances of that design working with another system are slight.

One area that shows great promise is *emulation*. Emulation is the art of making one device appear as if it were another. This has been used successfully with micro-to-mainframe connections. In place of the usual mainframe terminal is a personal computer.

Inside the desktop computer is a gateway package that makes the micro look and act like a standard terminal when viewed by the mainframe. It does this using protocol conversion. The gateway takes the micro's language and changes it into mainframe commands (and vice versa), thus giving the micro user the best of both worlds—local processing power with mainframe support.

The proliferation of incompatible networks, locally, nationally, and internationally, makes networking between dissimilar networks essential. Gateways, therefore, are assured a place in future networks.

TRANSPARENCY

The structure of a local area network should be *transparent*, both to the hosts on the local subnetworks and to the "outside world," the outside world being other networks to which the local network may be connected via gateways. In other words, any node wanting to talk to another node need not have special knowledge of whether or not the recipient is on the same subnetwork. Ultimately, the data package is addressed to its destination and whether it has to pass through one or more bridges is decided by the networks involved. This is transparency.

At present, there is a distinction between subnetworking, with its bridges, and internetworking gateways. In subnetworking it is assumed that all protocols are identical and that there is no substantial time lag between the execution of a message and its subsequent reception, other than "normal" network delay. Splitting a local area network into subnetworks has little impact on the key characteristics of the network. From a user's point of view, addressing is affected only slightly—if at all. The networks are totally transparent.

With gateway internetworking, on the other hand, the user must realize that the node to which the message is addressed is on a different network and that certain "unpackaging" and "repackaging" steps are involved before any communications are possible. Aggravating the situation is the fact that most gateways interconnect widely separated LANs, which forces them to translate through modems. A problem with modems, and network inter-

CAN I INTERFACE ONE NETWORK TO ANOTHER?

facing in general, is the matching of network speeds. A local area network operating at 10 megabits per second can load a 64K buffer in a twentieth of a second, whereas an intervening 9600-baud gateway requires nearly a minute to complete the same transmission. Similarly, it takes over two hours to transfer a 10-Mb file across the same bridge; that's assuming no other traffic is encountered. A low-delay service is clearly impossible under these circumstances.

In the future, you will see the distinction between subnetworking and internetworking becoming blurred. Transparency will creep into internetworking as the technology advances. Satellite communications will produce ever-increasing digital speeds, and the need for retransmission or acknowledgment will vanish with error-detecting and correction codes, thereby further improving throughput. It is speculated that one day it will be as easy to access data on other systems and networks as local access is today, and the entire globe will become one giant network.

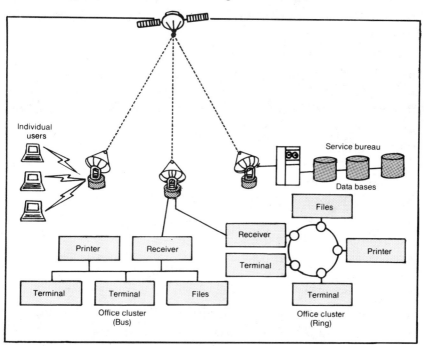

In the future you will see a trend toward more and more interconnecting of LANs. Satellite communications will provide the long-distance links, with dedicated land lines filling in the shorter hops. It is speculated that one day the entire globe will become a giant network.

13

SUPPOSE I NEED SECURITY?

We have all heard the horror stories about computer security or, more precisely, computer insecurity. The news media, television in particular, love to sensationalize computer break-in stories, generally those perpetrated by hackers who get their kicks from the challenge. Of course, such stories are made possible by the surge of computer networks getting online using public telephones and modems.

But hacking is more of a nuisance than anything else, and it is not the real computer security issue. The problem lies in the deliberate theft of sensitive information, such as project designs, proprietary formulas, market research, mailing lists, and cash flow schedules. This vital company information often represents millions of dollars. The loss of billing data or the distribution of trade secrets can be devastating to a company. In most cases, these crimes are committed not only by hackers, but by knowledgeable persons working within the intimate confines of an organization, or persons who have direct access to its computers.

Although you'd like implicitly to trust all your employees, you recognize that temptation is an overwhelming human frailty. As a result, companies are turning increasingly to computer security measures. Properly securing a local area network, though, raises a number of basic issues. Who should have access to the network, to which part of it, when, and how difficult should access be? And just how much security is actually necessary and at what cost? Oftentimes the answers are interrelated, so let's take it one step at a time.

SUPPOSE I NEED SECURITY?

Basically, the network user is faced with two security problems. First, there is the physical protection of the network against malicious attempts at entry, such as wiretapping. Second, and more prevalent, is the unauthorized use of the network and its contents.

At present, two schools of though prevail for protecting against unauthorized entry. The two policies are *discretionary security* and *mandatory security*.

DISCRETIONARY SECURITY

Discretionary security is the more open of the two policies. Discretionary policy assigns rules to the data files that specify who is allowed what type of access and to which objects. The assignment is made by the originator of the data. In other words, those who own a segment of data decide who can have access to it.

For example, suppose Jim, an employee of ACE Computer Company's legal department, needs a list of software department employees and their salaries in order to comply with affirmative action policies. This data is stored in the employee table of the personnel data base. The personnel administrator, Linda, grants him permission to retrieve this information by putting his name on her access list. At the same time, Linda restricts his queries just to the names and salaries of employees in the software department. She also decides to limit his access to the hours between 8 a.m. and 5 p.m. on weekdays only.

Now if Jim decides to stroll through company records, he can only dredge up the names and salaries of people working in the software department. If he wants to know what Becky in accounting is earning, he is out of luck unless he can coax it out of her personally. All other software-department-related information is also out of his grasp. Furthermore, Linda can cancel his access at any time by simply removing his name from the list.

Jim, of course, has a list of his own. Included in his files are the names of the personnel in the software department and what action, if any, is being planned for them. And, if policy dictates, Jim can prevent Linda from ever seeing his files—even though he may have access to hers, albeit limited.

119

MANDATORY SECURITY

By contrast, mandatory security implements the military view of security as a series of separate classifications—such as "secret" and "top secret"—to determine access. The network is built in hierarchical layers, with each classification occupying a layer. For entry to information contained in one of the layers, the subject must have a security clearance equal to or greater than the data itself.

Mandatory security can be implemented in either software or hardware. When using secure software, the network checks the validity of the user against a master clearance sheet. If the user's security level is equal to the hierarchical level requested, entry is permitted. The user may also access levels that are beneath his security clearance.

Unfortunately, this interaction between levels sometimes poses a problem. Through the use of a *Trojan horse* code, a lower level user could gain access to classified documents. A Trojan horse is a piece of code inserted into a trusted program that files data under many different names and files. A subverter, for instance, might place the Trojan horse into a text editor that is used by everyone at all levels. When a secret-level user is editing a secret file with the editor, the Trojan horse portion of the code instructs the program to copy the secret data into a low-priority file. Now all the thief has to do is glance into the file specified by the Trojan horse to view top-secret information.

USER	ACCESS TO	APPEND	REPLACE	DELETE
JIM	0800 TO 1700; MON TO FRI; DEPARTMENT D3	NONE	NONE	NONE
CARL	0800 TO 1700; MON TO FRI; DEPARTMENT D3, D4	0800 TO 1700; MON TO FRI; DEPARTMENT D3, D4	NONE	NONE
SUSAN	ALL	ALL	NONE	NONE
SANDY	ALL	ALL	D3	D3

Discretionary security is viewed as a software function. Essentially, a list is made of individuals who are allowed access to a file. Included in that list are the privileges and restrictions extended to each person. The assignment is made by the originator of the file. In other words, whoever owns the data decides who can have access to it.

SUPPOSE I NEED SECURITY?

Currently, the only way to protect the network from Trojan horse codes is to design it so that upper levels can't write into lower levels. This produces an upward flow of information as time progresses, and a trusted officer is needed to downgrade files that unwantedly creep into the upper levels.

Another approach to the mandatory security scheme is to separate the levels physically; that is, to have two (or more) LANs operating in the same space. While one LAN carries low-priority data, the other handles confidential material.

Separate local area networks can guarantee data security, but they also guarantee no network interoperability between levels. And unless the network users are rigidly cast, the system could grow into an unwieldy nightmare. When security levels overlap, more than one access terminal is needed. Not only is this messy, it is expensive. The designer's solution is to break the network into zones.

Suppose that in a 10-story building we were able to move all the top-secret users to the 10th floor. We can now easily install two separate local area networks into the building, one for the 10th

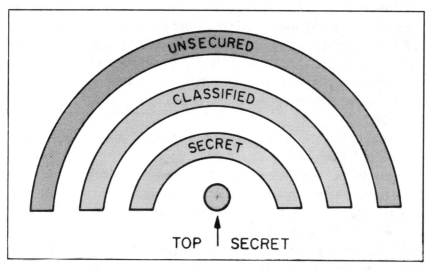

Mandatory security implements the military version of the security as a series of separate classifications. The network is built in hierarchical layers, with each classification occupying a layer. Entry is permitted to a user with a security clearance equal to or greater than a security level being accessed. Mandatory security can be installed using either software or hardware techniques.

floor and one for the lower nine levels. The installation is clean and simple with no duplication of effort.

Network security is also very tight. Anyone wishing to access the general network can easily do so from any one of the first nine floors. To get into the top-security network, though, you must travel to the 10th floor. Despite the security achieved, this could prove inconvenient to a 10th-level worker who must obtain information from the lesser network.

To improve the situation, the two networks can be joined with a bridge. Unlike most network interfaces, though, this gateway is a *trusted bridge*. The bridge has been modified to accept and pass all data that flows from the lower nine floors to the 10th floor. No data, however, can flow from the 10th floor downward. Although this arrangement provides total security while making the interface transparent to the lower level personnel, it does present a problem. Low-level users can't know whether a message was received by the upper level or not. Not even acknowledgments can return.

To allow reliable, but limited, interaction between the two zones, a *guard* is installed. The guard intercepts high-level security acknowledgments and changes their security status to pass to the lower level. Taking the guard concept one step further, the high-level user could attach a low-priority tag to messages that need to be sent down the link. The guard now sorts through all the incoming messages, decides their security priority, and either passes or rejects them. All lower level messages, however, flow upward unimpeded.

Actual physical separation of the networks doesn't necessarily mandate the use of separate cables, however. Adequate separation can be achieved by using a broadband network and placing each network on a different channel. Interaction of the networks can be accomplished by installing a trusted-bridge frequency converter at the network's head end. The converter transposes the frequencies of the channels so that the two networks can communicate.

TELEPHONE SECURITY

Telephone security poses a very special problem for local area networks. The very fact that you are using a public utility to transport data is like extending an open invitation to every hacker in town to try his or her hand at breaching your security. To make matters worse, your interface must be friendly enough that it doesn't take an act of Congress to gain authorized access. These, of course, are conflicting requirements.

One of the simplest and oldest tricks for protecting a direct-dial network is to use an unpublished telephone number. This very effectively prevents unwanted persons from dialing into your system "just for fun." Unfortunately, in today's computer society this is not a high-security solution. Even a simple computer equipped with a communications program and the proper modem can be used to dial phone numbers at random and identify those numbers that answer with the conventional modem carrier tone. An unlisted number is useless against this organized attack.

The most popular and well-known security method used today is the password system. This software technique denies access to the network to anyone without the proper password. The password, like an unlisted phone number, is kept secret and often is changed periodically to frustrate invasion attempts. But like the unlisted phone number, the password is vulnerable to systematic computer searches.

Through trial and error, a patient computer hacker can gain access to a network by running though a list of passwords one by one until a word is found that matches. In fact, the major problem with the password method is that users often assign very simple and easy-to-remember passwords to their files—words that are often duplicated and easy to guess. And the odds of finding the correct solution favor the intruder as time passes.

An obvious improvement over the simple password method is to restrict the number of tries one caller is permitted. Let's say that after the caller's third unsuccessful attempt at guessing the password, the network simply hangs up. This allows a legitimate user enough time to gain composure, yet is short enough to dampen the spirits of most hackers. To keep the intruder from dialing again and testing three more passwords, the network can be programmed to demand identification from the caller before it is willing to accept the passwords. Any caller who persistently issues invalid passwords will automatically be denied further communications. The caller's name can either be listed in permanent memory or logged on as the call comes in.

When the name is contained in memory, the network can verify the caller's identity and suspend communications immediately if the name isn't legitimate. Or, as some network owners have suggested, allow the intruder access to nonsense files for long enough to trace the telephone number and identify the culprit—or at least make the culprits *think* you know who they are. This is not

The most popular and lauded security technique used today is the password system. The password—like an unlisted phone number—is kept secret, and the network denies passage to anyone incapable of announcing the correct entry word. Unfortunately, the password is vulnerable to systematic computer searches, with the odds of guessing the word favoring the intruder as time passes. An obvious way to deter persistent attempts at guessing the password is to limit the number of tries one caller is permitted.

SUPPOSE I NEED SECURITY?

as silly as it sounds. Many liquor and department stores still employ dummy video cameras to scare off potential shoplifters. And how is a hacker to know if you're bluffing or not when a "TRACING PHONE CALL" message pops up on the display?

Given enough time, though, even this security scheme can be breached. You must remember, most hackers and thieves have nothing better to do than wait for your system to give a positive response. Of course, the harder you make it, the less willing a hacker will be to waste time on you. There are always easier pickings down the road.

Nevertheless, anyone who really wants in badly enough will eventually find a key that fits. *Callback security* is the latest effort to combat this practice. The callback idea is really quite simple.

Instead of answering the phone with the normal modem carrier tone, the callback modem answers all calls with silence. The caller is prompted, instead, to enter a verification code, usually using conventional Touch-Tone frequencies. Inside the modem's memory is a nonvolatile list of authorized users and their phone numbers. If the identity code matches one contained in the user memory, the modem responds with an acknowledgment tone, and both the caller and the modem disconnect.

In a normal callback situation, the network then dials the number of the person identified in the directory. The caller picks up the phone with a conventional modem carrier signal, and the two modems return handshakes. Access to the network is now secured.

Notice that callers cannot access a network from an unauthorized location—*even if they have an authorized code*—because the network dials the number stored in memory and the caller can't transfer that number to another location over the phone. For an even more secure system, the network can demand that the caller give further proof of identification after modem handshaking, such as a password or ID number, before allowing complete access. In fact, all the security techniques discussed in this chapter, hardware and software alike, can be mixed or matched.

ENCRYPTION

The ultimate in data security, however, is *encryption*—the art of secretly encoding messages. Secret codes have been used since ancient times. Hebrew scholars used codes to hide the Old Testament writings from the uninitiated, and Julius Caesar communicated with his troops in cryptogram.

The theory of cryptography is based on two operations: the substitution and transposition of characters in a word. In substitution, the binary bits are replaced with coded strings of bits. The substitution pattern is determined by a *key*. For instance, the key A=XR, B=GV, C=ES, D=PY transforms the word ABCD into XRGESPY. Notice how each original letter is replaced by two coded letters.

The transposition part of the process rearranges the order of the bits in the word, thereby changing its spelling. It, too, uses a key. For the transposition key 4132, ABCD becomes DACB. In other words, the fourth letter (D) is moved to the first position, the first letter is shifted to the second and so forth.

DATA ENCRYPTION STANDARD

Although some binary-encryption methods use proprietary keys to encode data, most U.S. manufacturers base their systems on the Data Encryption Standard (DES) algorithm developed by IBM and adopted by the National Bureau of Standards in 1976. DES is a product cipher code because it combines both cryptographic operations, substitution and transposition, to convert *plaintext* into *ciphertext*.

DES encrypts data eight bytes (64 bits) at a time. The plaintext word is first split into two and divided into left and right halves. The halves are then transposed. The left data block is processed through an algorithm that is steered by a 56-bit secret key. This secret key is user-identified and entered at the time of the encryption. The result of this calculation is 16 internal keys that will be used later. The right side of the plaintext works its way through a signal-processing network, where bits are substituted and transposed according to rules laid down by one of the internal keys.

126

SUPPOSE I NEED SECURITY?

This process is repeated 16 times, with each new encoding going back to the first step and accessing a new internal key. The end result is divided into halves again and transposed to restore left-right symmetry to the word. To decode a word, the same process is used, but in reverse order. A different key, will, of course, alter the order in which the substitution and transposition takes place.

DES has a number of features that make it especially hard to break. For one, the internal keys are nonlinear, in contrast to the

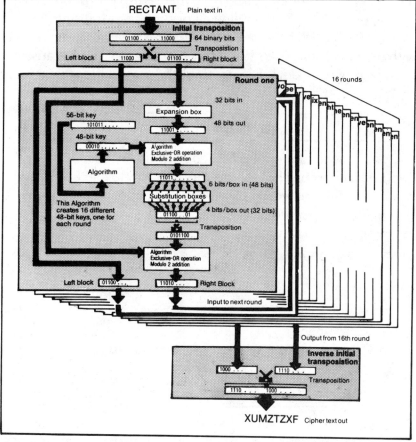

The ultimate in data security is data encryption, the art of security coding messages. The theory supporting cryptography is the substitution and transposition of characters in a word. The Data Encryption Standard (DES) is the most popular encryption method and is identified as a product cipher because it combines both encryption operations.

DES repeats substitution and transposition, one after the other, for sixteen rounds. Unraveling the secret message is accomplished by reversing the order of the substitutions and transpositions. A secret key determines their order, and the same key must be used for both operations. There are over a million billion possible key combinations.

127

rest of the DES operations which are linear. This makes it virtually impossible to derive the secret key using plaintext and ciphertext comparisons. And since the DES algorithm uses a 56-bit key, there are 7×10^{16} possible encryption combinations—no small number if you are using trial and error in searching for the secret key.

If additional security is required, several techniques can be called upon to further enhance DES security. An easy way to increase security without reducing data throughput is to perform the DES algorithm in reverse. That is, data is first enciphered by the sender using the DES decoding algorithm, then transmitted. The coded message is unraveled at the receiver by processing the data with the encrypting algorithm. This technique works because the enciphering and deciphering algorithms are mirror images of each other.

PUBLIC KEY

One disadvantage of the DES code is distribution of the secret key. Both users must have the same secret key to make the systems work. Whether delivered physically or electronically, this operation invites interception.

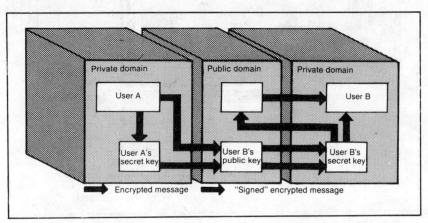

In public-key systems each user has two mathematically related keys—a public key that is listed in a directory and a secret key that is known only to the user. Secret messages are encoded with the receiver's public key. For instance, when user A sends a secret message to user B, the data is encoded using B's public key.

The only way to decode the message now is with user B's secret key, which is known only to him. Even A can't retrieve the original plaintext once encoded. A message to user A, on the other hand, is encoded with A's public code; a message to user C is done with C's public key.

SUPPOSE I NEED SECURITY?

An alternative encoding scheme that eliminates the distribution of the code key is the *public key* method. Public key systems employ two keys for each user—a public encryption key and a secret decryption key. The public keys are listed in a general directory that is distributed to all network users. The secret key is maintained by the user, and it is unique from any other secret key. No two are alike and only the immediate user knows it.

Secret messages are sent using the public key listed in the public directory. For example, when user A sends a secret message to user B, the data is encoded using B's public key. The only way to decode the message now is with user B's secret key, which is known only to him. Even A can't retrieve the original plaintext. Likewise, a secret message from B to A begins with user B looking up the public code for A and encrypting the message. A message to user C is done with C's public code.

Public-key systems are based on a one-way mathematical "trapdoor." The concept is that it is easier to work a formula in one direction than to try and solve it from the opposite direction. For example, it is easy to multiply two large prime numbers to get a large composite number, but it is extremely difficult to factor a composite back into its prime components.

Of course, either encryption method is suitable for general use inside or outside a local area network. Inside the network, the encrypting scheme could be used to divide a single network into hierarchical layers. While general data flowed through the network at the plaintext level, secret messages could flow through the same network in ciphertext, and only those possessing the proper key could read them. In fact, several layers could be present on one network with interoperability taking place at the plaintext level. Outside the LAN, the benefits are obvious.

SECURITY COMMON SENSE

Security in a local area network is hard to achieve and usually far from complete. The task is made easier if a few simple precautions are observed from the start. A software security auditor is commonly used in this type of practice.

The security auditor records successful and unsuccessful attempts at network access. The records should also include such activities as user identity, files accessed, interprocess messages, time in and time out. The auditory log can be used to detect illegal activities before they become a problem.

Obviously, your security is no better than your overall tidiness. Passwords that are left in computers long after their usefulness has expired are but one example of sloppy housekeeping. Another important aspect of secure systems is the removal of outdated information. Memory segments must be wiped clean before they are released for general distribution so that they contain no residue for anyone to browse through. Above all, keep confidential disks locked up at all times. There's little point in paying good money for security when anyone can stuff a diskette into a pocket and walk out the door with it.

Voice and fingerprint-recognition techniques may be the way of the future. For direct-access connection, voice recognition may prove to be the most secure of all identification techniques; fingerprints are more applicable to in-house use. In either case, the fundamental purpose is the same—user identification.

14

WHAT IS COMMERCIALLY AVAILABLE?

This book just wouldn't be complete, somehow, if I didn't tell you where you can buy a local area network. So here it is. A listing of LANs, as they exist in late 1984.

The following local area network list was supplied by the hardware-software directory of Data Sources, an information service of Ziff-Davis. As you will note, the listings provide a very comprehensive look at the many networks on the market and take a lot of the guesswork out of searching for a suitable LAN.

Data Sources' two-volume directory includes detailed descriptions for over 38,000 hardware and software products and contains profiles on 8600 companies. Data Sources is updated and published quaterly. These listings came from the 1984 third quarter edition. For further information contact Data Sources at 20 Brace Road, Cherry Hill, New Jersey 08034. (609-492-2100). To expedite an order you can call, toll-free, (800) 227-1617, extension 251. In California, call (800) 772-3545, extension 251.

MANUFACTURERS AND MODELS	PAGE NO.	TOPOLOGY						MGMT.			GATEWAYS						
		PHYSICAL RING (SERIES)	BUS	PHYSICAL RING (ADDRESS)	LOGICAL RING	STAR	OTHER	TOKEN PASSING	CSMA/CD	OTHER	BSC	SDLC	HDLC	SNA	X.25	ETHERNET	OTHER
ALSPA COMPUTER																	
Alspa-Net	140		•						•				•				
AMECOM																	
Government/Military UBITS (Universal Bus Information Transfer System)	140		•						•								•
APOLLO COMPUTER																	
DOMAIN Distributed Operating Multi-Access Interactive Network	140		•	•				•									•
APPLE COMPUTER																	
AppleNet	140		•	•					•							•	
APPLITEK																	
UniLINK	140		•					•	•	•	•	•	•		•		
AST RESEARCH																	
AST-PCnet	140		•						•		•						•
AST-PCnet II	140		•						•		•						
AUTOCONTROL																	
AUTOLAN	140		•						•			•					
CENTRAM SYSTEMS																	
The WEB	141		•						•							•	
CODEX																	
4000 Series LAN	141		•						•								

MANUFACTURERS AND MODELS	PAGE NO.	TOPOLOGY						MGMT.			GATEWAYS						
		PHYSICAL RING (SERIES)	BUS	PHYSICAL RING (ADDRESS)	LOGICAL RING	STAR	OTHER	TOKEN PASSING	CSMA/CD	OTHER	BSC	SDLC	HDLC	SNA	X.25	ETHERNET	OTHER
COMPLEXX SYSTEMS																	
XLAN	141		•						•								
COMPUTER AUTOMATION COMMERCIAL SYSTEMS DIVISION																	
SyFAnet	141		•						•			•	•				
COMPUTER AUTOMATION NAKED MINI DIVISION																	
OMNIX	141		•					•									
CONCORD DATA SYSTEMS																	
Token/Net	141		•		•		•	•									
CONTEL INFORMATION SYSTEMS																	
ConTelNet	141		•				•	•									
CORVUS SYSTEMS																	
Corvus Omninet	141		•				•		•					•			
CR COMPUTER SYSTEMS																	
X-Net	142		•				•		•	•	•			•	•		•
CROMEMCO																	
C-Net	142		•						•								
DATA GENERAL																	
XODIAC Network Bus (NBS)	142	•	•						•							•	
DATAPOINT																	
ARCnet (Attached Resource Computer System)	142		•	•	•				•			•	•	•			•

MANUFACTURERS AND MODELS	PAGE NO.	TOPOLOGY						MGMT.			GATEWAYS						
		PHYSICAL RING (SERIES)	BUS	PHYSICAL RING (ADDRESS)	LOGICAL RING	STAR	OTHER	TOKEN PASSING	CSMA/CD	OTHER	BSC	SDLC	HDLC	SNA	X.25	ETHERNET	OTHER
DAVONG SYSTEMS																	
MultiLink	142						●	●									
THE DESTEK GROUP																	
DESNET	142	●					●			●						●	
DEVELCON ELECTRONICS																	
Develnet	143						●								●	●	
DIGITAL EQUIPMENT																	
DEC Ethernet	143	●							●					●		●	●
DECdataway	143	●	●						●							●	●
DIGITAL MICROSYSTEMS																	
HiNet	143	●								●	●						
FOX RESEARCH																	
10-NET	143	●								●							
GANDALF DATA																	
PACXNET	143				●	●				●					●		●
GATEWAY COMMUNICATIONS																	
G/NET	143	●								●	●	●	●	●	●	●	●
GENERAL ELECTRIC MICROWAVE PRODUCTS DEPARTMENT																	
GEMLINK Digital Microwave Transmission System	143						●			●							
GEMLINK LSD-072A	144						●			●							

MANUFACTURERS AND MODELS	PAGE NO.	TOPOLOGY						MGMT.			GATEWAYS						
		PHYSICAL RING (SERIES)	BUS	PHYSICAL RING (ADDRESS)	LOGICAL RING	STAR	OTHER	TOKEN PASSING	CSMA/CD	OTHER	BSC	SDLC	HDLC	SNA	X.25	ETHERNET	OTHER
GEMLINK LSD-082A	143						●		●								
GEMLINK LSD-092A	143						●		●								
GEMLINK LSD-112A	143						●		●								
GEMLINK LSD-122A	143						●		●								
GENERAL TELENET																	
ETHERCOM	144	●							●							●	
GOULD PROGRAMMABLE CONTROL DIVISION																	
MODWAY	144	●		●				●									●
HARRIS DISTRIBUTED OFFICE SYSTEMS DIVISION																	
HNET Campus Link	144						●	●						●			●
HNET Work Group Link	144	●						●						●			●
IBM																	
PC LAN	145	●						●									
IDEAS																	
IDEAS LAN	145	●						●			●	●	●	●			
INFOTRON SYSTEMS																	
Local Area Network	145				●												
INTECOM																	
LANmark Integrated LAN for IBX Communication Systems	145				●					●						●	●
INTERACTIVE SYSTEMS/3M																	
ALAN (Advanced Local Area Network)	145	●					●	●									●

MANUFACTURERS AND MODELS	PAGE NO.	TOPOLOGY						MGMT			GATEWAYS						
		PHYSICAL RING (SERIES)	BUS	PHYSICAL RING (ADDRESS)	LOGICAL RING	STAR	OTHER	TOKEN PASSING	CSMA/CD	OTHER	BSC	SDLC	HDLC	SNA	X.25	ETHERNET	OTHER
VIDEODATA	145		•						•								
VIDEODATA LAN/I	145				•			•									
INTERPHASE																	
LNC 5180	145		•		•			•				•	•				
INTERSIL SYSTEMS																	
GEnet	146		•					•									•
KEYBROOK																	
The Network	146		•					•								•	
LANTECH SYSTEMS																	
Switch Board	146				•											•	
M/A-COM LINKABIT																	
IDX 30	146				•												•
M. A. SYSTEMS																	
Comnet	146	•															
MAGNOLIA MICROSYSTEMS																	
MAGNet	146		•		•			•									
MICOM SYSTEMS																	
INSTANET	146						•		•						•		
MICRO FIVE																	
Series 10 LAN	147				•												
MORROW DESIGNS																	
Morrow Network	147		•														

MANUFACTURERS AND MODELS	PAGE NO.	TOPOLOGY						MGMT.			GATEWAYS						
		PHYSICAL RING (SERIES)	BUS	PHYSICAL RING (ADDRESS)	LOGICAL RING	STAR	OTHER	TOKEN PASSING	CSMA/CD	OTHER	BSC	SDLC	HDLC	SNA	X.25	ETHERNET	OTHER
NBI																	
NBI Net	147		●						●								
NCR																	
Mirlan	147		●						●								
NESTAR SYSTEMS																	
PLAN 20	147		●					●									
PLAN 30	147		●					●									●
PLAN 40	147		●				●	●									●
NETWORK SYSTEMS																	
HYPERbus	147		●							●							
HYPERchannel	147		●							●							●
NORTH STAR COMPUTERS																	
NorthNet	147		●							●							●
NOVELL																	
NETWARE/S	148				●	●				●					●	G	●
NETWARE/X	148		●														
ORCHID TECHNOLOGY																	
PCNET	148		●						●								
PERCOM DATA																	
Percomnet	148					●	●		●							●	●
PRAGMATRONICS																	
TIENET	148		●				●		●	●	●		●				
PRIME COMPUTER																	
RINGNET	148			●				●									●

MANUFACTURERS AND MODELS	PAGE NO.	TOPOLOGY						MGMT.			GATEWAYS						
		PHYSICAL RING (SERIES)	BUS	PHYSICAL RING (ADDRESS)	LOGICAL RING	STAR	OTHER	TOKEN PASSING	CSMA/CD	OTHER	BSC	SDLC	HDLC	SNA	X.25	ETHERNET	OTHER
PROLINK																	
PROloop	148	●	●			●			●	●	●						
PROTEON																	
proNET Star-Shaped Ring	149			●		●			●			●			●		●
RACAL-MILGO																	
Planet	149					●		●									
SCIENTIFIC DATA SYSTEMS																	
SDSNET	149					●			●								
SD SYSTEMS																	
MARS/Net	149	●	●					●									
SIECOR																	
Fiberlan-Net 10	149	●			●			●								●	
SPACE COAST SYSTEMS																	
PC-LINK	149				●												
STANDARD DATA																	
Disc-less Network	150	●						●							●	●	
STARNET DATA SYSTEMS																	
Starnet II	150				●				●								
STEARNS COMPUTER SYSTEMS																	
MICRONETWORK	150				●												
STRATUS COMPUTER																	
StrataLink	150			●						●	●	●	●				

MANUFACTURERS AND MODELS	PAGE NO.	TOPOLOGY						MGMT.			GATEWAYS						
		PHYSICAL RING (SERIES)	BUS	PHYSICAL RING (ADDRESS)	LOGICAL RING	STAR	OTHER	TOKEN PASSING	CSMA/CD	OTHER	BSC	SDLC	HDLC	SNA	X.25	ETHERNET	OTHER
SYDIS																	
SYLINK	150					•			•		•	•	•	•	•		
SYTEK																	
LocalNet	150	•						•	•		•				•	•	
TECMAR																	
ComNet	150		•	•					•								
TRANTOR SYSTEMS																	
The Web	151					•		•			•	•	•				
UNGERMANN-BASS																	
Net/One	151	•							•							•	•
VECTOR GRAPHIC																	
LINC	151		•					•			•						
WANG LABORATORIES																	
WangNet	151		•	•			•		•	•							•
WESTERN DIGITAL																	
NetSource/PC-LAN	151				•			•									
WINSOURCE																	
Winnet	151				•			•									
XCOMP																	
X-Net	151	•															
XEROX																	
Ethernet	152		•	•					•								
XYPLEX																	
The XYPLEX System	152	•							•								

LOCAL NETWORKS

ALSPA COMPUTER, INC.

Alspa Computer, Inc.
477 Division St.
Campbell, CA. 95008
(408) 370-3000 Est. 1981

● Alspa-Net

Bus ☐ Baseband ☐ Contention (CSMA/CD)
☐ Central controller required ☐ CPU: TUR-
BODOS ☐ Twisted pair cable ☐ 256 connections ☐ 800K bps max. ☐ 2,000 ft. max.
distance ☐ HDLC gateway(s) ☐ 150 installed ☐ 1982 ☐ Pricing — $1,995

AMECOM

Amecom
(division of Litton Systems, Inc.)
5115 Calvert Rd.
College Park, MD 20740
(301) 864-5600 Est. 1964

● Government/Military UBITS
(Universal Bus Information
Transfer System)

Bus ☐ Baseband ☐ Contention (CSMA/CD)
☐ CPU: Equipment transparent ☐ Twisted
pair cable; Optical fiber ☐ Up to 16K active
connections ☐ 160M bps max. ☐ 1,000 ft.
max. distance ☐ RS-232; RS-423; MIL 188C
interface(s) ☐ OSI Level 4 gateway(s) ☐ 4
installed ☐ 1982

APOLLO COMPUTER, INC.

Apollo Computer, Inc.
330 Billerica Rd.
Chelmsford, MA 01824
(617) 256-6600 Est. 1980

● DOMAIN Distributed Operating
Multi-Access Interactive Network

Bus; Physical ring (addressing) ☐ Baseband ☐ Token passing (statistical polling) ☐
CPU: 32-bit ☐ Coaxial cable ☐ Several hundred connections ☐ 12M bps max. ☐ 1 kilometer between nodes max. distance ☐
IEEE-488 interface(s) ☐ Other DOMAIN
rings; IBM gateway(s) ☐ 3,000 installed ☐
1981

APPLE COMPUTER, INC.

Apple Computer, Inc.
20525 Mariani Ave., Mail Stop 23AD
Cupertino, CA 95014
(408) 973-3152 Est. 1977

● AppleNet

Bus; Physical ring (addressing) ☐ Contention (CSMA/CD) ☐ CPU: Apple Personal
Computers ☐ 128 connections ☐ 1M bps
max. ☐ 2,000 ft. max. distance ☐ Ethernet
gateway(s) ☐ 1983

APPLITEK CORP.

Applitek Corp.
107 Audubon Rd.
Wakefield, MA 01880
(617) 246-4500 Est. 1982

● UniLINK

Bus; Tree ☐ Broadband; Baseband; Fiber
Optic ☐ Token passing (statistical polling);
Contention (CSMA/CD) ☐ CPU: Motorola
6800 ☐ Coaxial cable; Optical fiber ☐ Base-
band-1,000; Broadband-40,000; Optical Fi-
ber-1,000 connections ☐ 10M bps max. ☐
Broadband-30 kilometers; Baseband-2.5
kilometers; Optical Fiber-30 kilometers max.
distance ☐ IEEE-488; RS-232; RS-449 inter-
face(s) ☐ BSC; SDLC; HDLC; X.25 gate-
way(s) ☐ 1984

AST RESEARCH, INC.

AST Research, Inc.
2121 Alton Ave.
Irvine, CA 92714
(714) 863-1333 Est. 1981

● AST-PCnet

Bus ☐ Baseband ☐ Contention (CSMA/CD)
☐ CPU: IBM PC, XT/PCDOS and compatibles ☐ Coaxial cable ☐ 238 connections ☐
800K bps max. ☐ 5,000 ft. max. distance ☐
BSC; Async gateway(s) ☐ 1983 ☐ Pricing —
$695 per node

● AST-PCnet II

Bus ☐ Baseband ☐ Contention (CSMA/CD)
☐ CPU: IBM PC ☐ Twisted pair cable ☐ 160
connections ☐ 800K bps max. ☐ 2,500 ft.
max. distance ☐ BSC gateway(s) ☐ 1984

AUTOCONTROL, INC.

Autocontrol, Inc.
11400 Dorsett Rd.
St. Louis, MO 63043
(314) 739-0055 Est. 1970

WHAT IS COMMERCIALLY AVAILABLE?

• AUTOLAN

Bus ☐ Baseband ☐ Contention (CSMA/CD) ☐ CPU: IBM PC ☐ Coaxial cable ☐ 255 connections ☐ 848K bps max. ☐ 7,000 ft. max. distance ☐ SDLC gateway(s) ☐ 50 installed ☐ 1983 ☐ Pricing — $250

CENTRAM SYSTEMS, INC.

Centram Systems, Inc.
Sleepy Hollow RD2
Etters, PA 17319
(717) 763-1198 Est.1982

• The WEB

Bus ☐ Baseband ☐ Contention (CSMA/CD) ☐ Four connector telco-cable ☐ 64 connections ☐ 500K bps max. ☐ 2,000 ft. max. distance ☐ RS-422 interface(s) ☐ Ethernet gateway(s) ☐ 200 installed ☐ 1983 ☐ Pricing — $350

CODEX CORP.

Codex Corp.
(subsidary of Motorola, Inc.)
20 Cabot Blvd.
Mansfield, MA 02048
(617) 364-2000 Est. 1962

• 4000 Series LAN

Bus ☐ Broadband; Baseband ☐ Contention (CSMA/CD) ☐ Coaxial cable ☐ 10M bps max. ☐ 500 meters max. distance ☐ IEEE-488; RS-232 interface(s) ☐ 1984 ☐ Pricing — $450-$750 per port

COMPLEXX SYSTEMS, INC.

Complexx Systems, Inc.
4930 Research Dr.
Huntsville, AL 35805
(205) 830-4310 Est. 1982

• XLAN

Bus ☐ Baseband ☐ CSMA ☐ Twisted pair cable ☐ 64 connections ☐ 1M bps max. ☐ 10,000 ft. max. distance ☐ RS-232 interface(s) ☐ 1983 ☐ Pricing — $362/connection

COMPUTER AUTOMATION, INC.

Computer Automation, Inc.
Commercial Systems Division
1800 Jay E11 Dr.
Richardson, TX 75081
(214) 783-0993 Est. 1975

• SyFAnet

Bus ☐ Broadband ☐ CSMA/CA ☐ Coaxial cable ☐ 64 connections ☐ 3M bps max. ☐ 3,000 ft. max. distance ☐ RS-232 interface(s) ☐ SNA; X.25 gateway(s) ☐ 7 installed ☐ 1983 ☐ Pricing — $4,000-$8,600

COMPUTER AUTOMATION, INC.

Computer Automation, Inc.
Naked Mini Division
18651 Von Karman
Irvine, CA 92713
(714) 833-8830 Est. 1967

• OMNIX

Bus ☐ Contention (CSMA/CD) ☐ CPU: CA OMNIX ☐ Twisted pair cable ☐ 60 connections ☐ 400K bps max. ☐ RS-232 interface(s) ☐ 1983

CONCORD DATA SYSTEMS, INC.

Concord Data Systems, Inc.
303 Bear Hill Rd.
Waltham, MA 02154
(617) 890-1394 Est. 1981

• Token/Net

Bus; Logical ring; Meets IEEE 802-4 ☐ Broadband ☐ Token passing (statistical polling) ☐ CPU: Vendor independent ☐ Coaxial cable ☐ Over 1,000 connections ☐ 5M bps max. ☐ Over 25 miles max. distance ☐ IEEE-488; RS-232; RS-449 interface(s) ☐ 1983 ☐ Pricing — $500-$2,000/connection

CONTEL INFORMATION SYSTEMS, INC.

Contel Information Systems, Inc.
(subsidary of Continental Telecom, Inc)
130 Steamboat Rd.
Great Neck, NY 11024
(516) 829-5900 Est. 1982

• ConTelNet

Bus; Tree ☐ Broadband; Baseband ☐ Contention (CSMA/CD) ☐ Coaxial cable ☐ Unlimited connections ☐ 2M bps; 10M bps max. ☐ 5 mile radius max. distance ☐ RS-232; BSC; HDLC; TTY interface(s) ☐ X.25 gateway(s) ☐ 25 installed ☐ 1980 ☐ Pricing — $438/connection

CORVUS SYSTEMS, INC.

Corvus Systems, Inc.
2920 O'Toole Ave.
San Jose, CA 95131
(408) 946-7700 Est. 1979

• Corvus Omninet

Bus; Bus with Branching □ Baseband □ Contention (CSMA/Collision Avoidance); Positive Acknowledgement □ CPU: Apple II, III; DEC LSI-11, Rainbow 100; IBM PC; Corvus Concept; Zenith Z 100 Series; TI Professional □ Twisted pair cable □ 64 connections □ 1M bps max. □ 4,000 ft. max. distance □ Corvus Transporter (RS-422 on network side) interface(s) □ SNA gateway(s) □ 6,000 installed □ 1981 □ Pricing — $500/connection

CR COMPUTER SYSTEMS, INC.

CR Computer Systems, Inc.
(subsidary of Christian Rovsing A/S)
5456 McConnell Ave., Suite 182
Los Angeles, CA   90066
(213) 822-5112   Est. 1963

• X-Net

Bus; Branch rooted tree □ Baseband □ Roll call polling □ Central controller required □ CPU: IBM 43XX, 30XX, 370, PC/XT; DEC PDP, VAX; HP 3000; NCR; Honeywell; Univac □ Twisted pair cable □ 255 sites, each 2,032 node connections □ 14.746M bps max. □ 4,000 meters (2.5 miles) max. distance □ RS-232; Multibus interface(s) □ BSC; HDLC; X.25; X.21; SNA/SDLC gateway(s) □ 72 installed □ 1978 □ Pricing — $1,000-$1,200

CROMEMCO, INC.

Cromemco, Inc.
280 Bernardo Ave.
Mountain View, CA   94039
(415) 964-7400   Est. 1976

• C-Net

Bus □ Baseband □ Contention (CSMA/CD) □ Central controller required □ CPU: Z80A; 68000 □ Twisted pair cable □ 255 connections □ 880K bps max. □ 2,000 meter separation between stations max. distance □ 1982 □ Pricing — $1,000 per single-user node

DATA GENERAL CORP.

Data General Corp.
4400 Computer Dr.
Westboro, MA   01581
(617) 366-8911   Est. 1968

• XODIAC Network Bus (NBS)

Bus; Physical ring (addressing) □ Broadband □ Token passing (statistical polling) □ CPU: Data General ECLIPSE □ Coaxial cable □ 32 connections □ 2M bps max. □ 1 mile max. distance □ X.25 gateway(s) □ 1981 □ Pricing — $3,400 basic CPU to cable

DATAPOINT CORP.

Datapoint Corp.
9725 Datapoint Dr., Suite MST-47
San Antonio, TX   78284
(512) 699-7000   Est. 1968

• ARCnet (Attached Resource Computer System)

Bus; Logical ring; Star □ Baseband □ Polling □ CPU: Datapoint ARC □ Coaxial cable □ 255 device connections □ 2.5M bps max. □ 4 miles (2,000 ft. between active repeaters) max. distance □ RS-232; Datapoint RIM (Resource Interface Module) interface(s) □ SNA; HDLC; X.25; TLX; TWX gateway(s) □ 5,000 installed □ 1977

DAVONG SYSTEMS, INC.

Davong Systems , Inc.
217 Humboldt Court Dr.
Sunnyvale, CA   94089
(408) 734-4900   Est. 1961

• MultiLink

Unconstrained □ Broadband □ Token passing (statistical polling) □ CPU: IBM PC, XT and compatibles □ Coaxial cable □ 255 connections □ 2.5M bps max. □ 20,000 ft. between stations max. distance □ 2,000 nodes installed □ 1983 □ Pricing — $595 (interface card per node); $100 (4-connector hub); $800 (8-connector hub); $500 (software license)

THE DESTEK GROUP

The Destek Group
830 E. Evelyn Ave.
Sunnyvale, CA   94086
(408) 737-7211   Est. 1981

• DESNET

Bus; Logical ring (for fiberoptics only) □ Baseband; Broadband □ Contention (CSMA/CA) □ Coaxial cable; Optical fiber □ Over 350 connections □ 2M bps max. □ 2 kilometers max. distance □ IEEE-488; RS-232; 8 or 16-bit parallel; S-100 Bus; Multibus; IBM PC; Q-Bus interface(s) □ Ethernet gateway(s) □ 500 installed □ 1982 □ Pricing — $400-$600/connection

WHAT IS COMMERCIALLY AVAILABLE?

DEVELCON ELECTRONICS, INC.

Develcon Electronics, Inc.
4037 Swamp Rd.
Doylestown, PA 18901
(215) 348-1900 Est. 1978

● Develnet

Cluster ☐ Central controller required ☐ Twisted pair cable ☐ 240 (lines per node) connections ☐ 24M bps max. ☐ RS-232; RS-449 serial internode interface(s) ☐ X.25; Ethernet gateway(s) ☐ 1983

DIGITAL EQUIPMENT CORP.

Digital Equipment Corp.
146 Main St.
Maynard, MA 01754
(617) 897-5111 Est. 1957

● DEC Ethernet

Bus ☐ Baseband ☐ Contention (CSMA/CD) ☐ CPU: DEC PDP-11, VAX, Professional 300 Series, DECNet; Ethernet compatible with interfaces ☐ Coaxial cable ☐ 1,024 connections ☐ 10M bps max. ☐ 2.8 kilometers max. distance ☐ H4000 Transceiver interface(s) ☐ SNA; Ethernet; DECNet gateway(s) ☐ 1982 ☐ Pricing — $3,800/connection plus cables ($300 H4000)

● DECdataway

Bus; Physical ring (addressing) ☐ Baseband; Spatial bit-stuffing protocol ☐ Contention (CSMA/CD) ☐ CPU: DEC; Ethernet compatible ☐ Twisted pair cable; Coaxial cable ☐ 31 connections ☐ 10M bps max. ☐ 15,000 ft. max. distance ☐ Ethernet; DECnet gateway(s) ☐ 1982 ☐ Pricing — $1,400-$14,000/connection

DIGITAL MICROSYSTEMS, INC.

Digital Microsystems. Inc.
1840 Embarcadero
Oakland, CA 94606
(415) 532-3686 Est. 1974

● HiNet

Bus ☐ Baseband ☐ Master/slave ☐ Central controller required ☐ CPU: CP/M 80; CP/M 86 ☐ Twisted pair cable; Ribbon cable ☐ 32 connections ☐ 500K bps max. ☐ 1,000 ft. max. distance ☐ RS-232; RS-422 interface(s) ☐ SDLC gateway(s) ☐ 2,000 installed ☐ 1980 ☐ Pricing — $1,695 (DMS-1280 workstation); $11,990 (DMS-3/103 46M byte master station)

FOX RESEARCH, INC.

Fox Research, Inc.
7005 Corporate Way
Dayton, OH 45459
(513) 433-2238 Est. 1983

● 10-NET

Bus ☐ Baseband ☐ Contention (CSMA/CA) ☐ CPU: IBM PC and compatibles ☐ Twisted pair cable ☐ 32 connections ☐ 1M bps max. ☐ 2,000 feet max. distance ☐ 200 installed ☐ 1984 ☐ Pricing — $695 per node

GANDALF DATA, INC.

Gandalf Data, Inc.
(subsidary of Gandalf Tech., Inc.)
1019 S. Noel Ave.
Wheeling, IL 60090
(312) 541-6060 Est. 1973

● PACXNET

Star; Node-to-node: Ring or full star ☐ Broadband; Baseband ☐ Contention ☐ Twisted pair cable; Coaxial cable; Optical fiber; Copper wire ☐ 1,500 per node; 4,000 per network connections ☐ 9,600 bps async; 19.2K bps sync; 5.3M bps intranode bus speed max. ☐ No physical limitations on max. distance ☐ RS-232; RS-422/423; Mil Std. 188-114; FED-STD-1030 interface(s) ☐ X.25; PBX; 3270 network gateway(s) ☐ 1982 ☐ Pricing — $100-$250 per port

GATEWAY COMMUNICATIONS, INC.

Gateway Communications, Inc.
16782 Redhill Ave.
Irvine, CA 92714
(714) 261-0762 Est. 1981

● G/NET

Bus ☐ Baseband ☐ Contention (CSMA/CD/CA) ☐ CPU: IBM PC and PC compatibles ☐ Coaxial cable ☐ 255 connections ☐ 1.43M bps max. ☐ 7,000 ft. max. distance ☐ BSC; SDLC; HDLC; SNA; X.25; Ethernet gateway(s) ☐ 811 installed ☐ 1983 ☐ Pricing — $595

GENERAL ELECTRIC CO.

General Electric Co.
Microwave Products Department
316 E. Ninth St.
Owensboro, KY 42301
(502) 685-6200 Est. 1981

● GEMLINK Digital Microwave Transmission System

143

Point-to-point ☐ Digital Baseband; BPSK ☐ Line Transparent ☐ CPU: Hardware independent ☐ K-band Microwave ☐ Multiplexor/switch dependent connections ☐ 3.152M bps max. ☐ Point-to-point line of sight up to 25 miles max. distance ☐ RS-232; RS-449/422; V.35; Bell 303; DSX-1; DSX-1C interface(s) ☐ 1,000 installed ☐ 1981 ☐ Pricing — $8,000-$20,000 (Interfaces with multiplexors; wireless system eliminates the need for modems and monthly leased-line costs for local loop situations under 25 miles)

● GEMLINK LSD-072A

Point-to-point ☐ Baseband; FSK ☐ Line transparent ☐ CPU: Hardware independent ☐ K-band Microwave ☐ Single async port connections ☐ 1.2-19.2K bps max. ☐ 10 miles max. distance ☐ RS-232 interface(s) ☐ 1981 ☐ Pricing — $5,000 (both ends)

● GEMLINK LSD-082A

Point-to-point ☐ Digital Baseband; FSK ☐ Line Transparent ☐ CPU: Hardware independent ☐ K-band Microwave ☐ Multiplexor dependent connections ☐ 19.2K bps max. ☐ 10 miles max. distance ☐ RS-232 interface(s) ☐ 1981 ☐ Pricing — $7,950 (both ends)

● GEMLINK LSD-092A

Point-to-point ☐ Digital Baseband; BPSK ☐ Line Transparent ☐ CPU: Hardware independent ☐ K-band Microwave ☐ Multiplexor dependent connections ☐ 300K bps max. ☐ 25 miles max. distance ☐ RS-449/442; V.35; Bell 303 interface(s) ☐ 1982 ☐ Pricing — $10,250 (both ends)

● GEMLINK LSD-112A

Point-to-point ☐ Digital Baseband; BPSK ☐ Line Transparent ☐ CPU: Hardware independent ☐ K-band Microwave ☐ Multiplexor dependent connections ☐ 3.152M bps max. ☐ 25 miles max. distance ☐ RS-449/442; DSX-1C interface(s) ☐ 1982 ☐ Pricing — $18,000 (both ends)

● GEMLINK LSD-122A

Point-to-point ☐ Digital Baseband; BPSK ☐ Line Transparent ☐ CPU: Hardware independent ☐ K-band Microwave ☐ Multiplexor/PBX dependent connections ☐ 1.544M or 2.048M bps max. ☐ 25 miles max. distance ☐ RS-449/442; DSX-1 interface(s) ☐ 1982 ☐ Pricing — $12,000 (both ends)

GENERAL TELENET, INC.

General Telenet, Inc.
212 East 47th St.
New York, NY 10017
(212) 644-6972 Est. 1980

● ETHERCOM

Bus ☐ Baseband ☐ Contention (CSMA/CD) ☐ Central controller required ☐ CPU: IBM PC ☐ Coaxial cable ☐ 1,000 connections ☐ 10M bps max. distance ☐ Ethernet gateway(s) ☐ 16 installed ☐ 1983 ☐ Pricing — $1,200

GOULD, INC.

Gould Inc.
Programmable Control Division
P.O. Box 3083
Andover, MA 01810
(617) 475-4700 Est. 1970

● MODWAY

Bus; Logical ring ☐ Broadband; Baseband ☐ Token passing (statistical polling) ☐ CPU: Gould Modicon ☐ Coaxial cable ☐ 256 (token owners) per segment connections ☐ 1.544M bps max. ☐ 15,000 ft. max. distance ☐ RS-232; Serial line interface(s) ☐ MODBUS; X.25 as ADCE gateway(s) ☐ 20 installed ☐ 1982 ☐ Pricing — $1,000-$5,000/connection

HARRIS CORP.

Harris Corp.
Distribution Office Systems Divisions
505 John Rodes Blvd.
Melbourne, FL 32901
(305) 242-5000 Est. 1982

● HNET Campus Link

Unconstrained ☐ Broadband ☐ Token passing (statistical polling) ☐ CPU: Harris ☐ Coaxial cable ☐ 254 device per ch. connections ☐ 10M bps max. ☐ SNA; 2780/3780 gateway(s) ☐ 1983

● HNET Work Group Link

Bus ☐ Baseband ☐ Token passing (statistical polling) ☐ Central controller required ☐ CPU: Harris 9000 Series ☐ Coaxial cable ☐ 32 connections ☐ 1M bps max. ☐ 5,000 ft. max. distance ☐ SNA; 2780/3780 gateway(s) ☐ 1983

WHAT IS COMMERCIALLY AVAILABLE?

IBM (INTERNATIONAL BUSINESS MACHINES)

IBM (International Business Machines)
Information Systems Group
National Accounts Division
Old Orchard Rd.
Armonk, NY 10504
(914) 765-9600 Est. 1914

● PC LAN

Bus □ Baseband □ Contention (CSMA/CD) □ CPU: IBM PC, XT, PCjr., PC portable computer □ Coaxial cable □ 64 connections □ 375K bps max. □ 3,230 ft. max. distance □ 1984

IDEAS, INC. (INFORMATION DEVELOPMENT AND APPLICATIONS, INC.)

Ideas, Inc. (Information Development and Applications, Inc.)
10759 Tucker St.
Beltsville, MD 20702
(301) 937-3600 Est. 1982

● IDEAS LAN

Bus □ Broadband □ Contention (CSMA/CD) □ CPU: Z80 □ Coaxial cable □ 4 per Bus Interface Unit (BIU) connections □ 1.544M bps max. □ Topology determines max. distance □ RS-232; RS-422; Mil Std. 188C interface(s) □ BSC; SDLC; HDLC; X.25 gateway(s) □ 1,200 installed □ 1981 □ Pricing — $600/connection (4-port model)

INFOTRON SYSTEMS CORP.

Infotron Systems Corps.
9 N. Olny Ave.
Cherry Hill, NJ 08003
(609) 424-9400 Ext. 6230 Est. 1968

● Local Area Network

Ring □ Central controller required □ Twisted pair cable □ 2,000 connections □ 64K bps max. □ 2,000 ft. between nodes max. distance □ RS-232 interface(s) □ 100 installed □ 1983 □ Pricing — $220

INTECOM, INC.

Intecom, Inc.
601 Intecom Dr.
Allen, TX 75002
(214) 727-9141 Ext. 2398 Est. 1979

● LANmark Integrated LAN for IBX Communication Systems

Star □ Broadband □ Proprietary □ Central controller required □ CPU: Perkin-Elmer 3205, 3210 □ Twisted pair cable □ 8,192 device connections □ 1M bps; Burst mode 10M bps max. □ Up to 10 miles between devices max. distance □ RS-232; RS-449; V.35; Ethernet; BNC coax interface(s) □ Ethernet; T-1; 3270 gateway(s) □ 1983 □ Pricing — $500 per user interface; $10,000 as a basic option to IBX (introductory pricing)

INTERACTIVE SYSTEMS/3M

Interactive Systems/3M
TelCom Products Division
3980 Varsity Dr.
Ann Arbor, MI 48104
(313) 973-1500 Est. 1969

● ALAN (Advanced Local Area Network)

Bus □ Broadband □ Token passing (statistical polling); Contention (CSMA/CD) □ Coaxial cable □ 5M bps max. □ RS-232 interface(s) □ TTY gateway(s) □ 250 installed □ 1972 □ Pricing — $1,995-$5,500/connection

● VIDEODATA

Bus □ Broadband □ Contention (CSMA/CD) □ CPU: IBM □ Coaxial cable □ 248 per ch. connections □ 100K bps per ch. max. □ 40 miles max. distance □ 1972 □ Pricing — $600-$900/connection

● VIDEODATA LAN/I

Logical ring □ Broadband □ Token passing (statistical polling) □ Coaxial cable □ 2,000 (per ch. pair) connections □ 2.5M bps max. □ NIU interface(s) □ 1983 □ Pricing — $360 per port/connection

INTERPHASE CORP.

Interphase Corp.
O.E.M. Products
2925 Merrell Rd.
Dallas, TX 75229
(214) 350-9000 Est. 1975

● LNC 5180

Bus; Star □ Broadband; Baseband □ Token passing (statistical polling) □ Twisted pair cable; Coaxial cable; Optical fiber □ 255 connections □ 2M bps (T1 compatible at 1.544M bps) max. □ 30,000 ft. max. distance □ Multibus interface(s) □ SDLC; HDLC gateway(s) □ 100 installed □ 1982 □ Pricing — $1,995/connection

INTERSIL SYSTEMS, INC.

Intersil Systems, Inc.
(subsidiary of General Electric Co.)
1275 Hammerwood Ave.
Sunnyvale, CA 91405
(408) 743-4300 Est. 1968

● GEnet

Bus □ Broadband □ Contention (CSMA/CD) □ Central controller required □ Coaxial cable □ 4 devices per BIU; 2,000 (per ch.) connections □ 1M bps max. □ RS-232; DR11W interface(s) □ DECNET gateway(s) □ 1983 □ Pricing — $10,000-$12,000 (minimum system 8 ports)

KEYBROOK

Keybrook
2035 National Ave.
Hayward, CA 94545
(415) 887-8999 Est. 1979

● The Network

Bus □ Baseband □ Contention (CSMA/CD) □ Central controller required □ CPU: CP/M; MSDOS □ Twisted pair cable □ 32 connections □ 307K bps max. □ 15 networks may be connected; 2,000 ft. per network max. distance □ IEEE-488 interface(s) □ Ethernet gateway(s) □ 150 installed □ 1982 □ Pricing — $300/connection

LANTECH SYSTEMS, INC.

Lantech Systems, Inc.
9635 Wendell Rd.
Dallas, TX 75243
(214) 340-4932 Est. 1983

● Switch Board

Star □ Baseband □ Central controller required □ CPU: IBM PC, XT □ Twisted pair cable □ 9 connections □ 250K bps max. □ 500 ft. max. distance □ RS-232; RS-422 interface(s) □ Ethernet gateway(s) □ 1984 □ Pricing — $400-$750

M/A-COM LINKABIT, INC.

M/A-COM Linkabit, Inc.
3033 Science Park Rd.
San Diego, CA 92121
(619) 457-2340 Est. 1968

● IDX 3000

Star □ Baseband; Bell T1, DS1 □ Central controller required □ Twisted pair cable; Microwave □ 3,072 line connections □ 19.2K bps per ch. max. □ 2 miles (3.1 sq. miles) max. distance □ RS-232; T1 interface(s) □ T1 gateway(s) □ 15 installed □ 1982 □ Pricing — $200/line

M. A. SYSTEMS, INC.

M.A. Systems, Inc.
2015 O'Toole Ave.
San Jose, CA 95131
(408) 943-0596 Est. 1980

● Comnet

Physical ring (series) □ Central controller required □ Coaxial cable □ 64 connections □ IEEE-488; RS-232 interface(s) □ 50 installed □ 1984

MAGNOLIA MICROSYSTEMS

Magnolia Microsystems
2264 15th Ave., W.
Seattle, WA 98119
(206) 285-7266 Est. 1978

● MAGNet

Bus; Logical ring □ Baseband □ Token passing (statistical polling) □ CPU: Z80; IBM PC compatibles □ Twisted pair cable □ 64 connections □ 500K bps max. □ 2,000 ft. max. distance □ RS-422 interface(s) □ 10 installed □ 1983 □ Pricing — $695

MICOM SYSTEMS, INC.

Micom Systems Inc.
20151 Nordhoff St.
Chatsworth, CA 91311
(818) 998-8844 Ext. 2572 Est. 1973

● INSTANET

Unconstrained □ Baseband □ Dedicated paths/Circuit switch □ Central controller required □ CPU: Z80A □ Twisted pair cable □ Configuration determines number of connections □ 1.544M bps max. □ 1 mile max. distance □ RS-232 interface(s) □ X.25 gateway(s) □ 1983 □ Pricing — $100-$575

WHAT IS COMMERCIALLY AVAILABLE?

MICRO FIVE CORP.

Micro Five Corp.
3560 Hyland Ave., P.O. Box 5011
Costa Mesa, CA 2626
(714) 957-1517 Est. 1977

● Series 1000 LAN

Star ☐ Baseband ☐ CPU: Micro Five Series 1000 ☐ Twisted pair cable ☐ 11 user connections ☐ RS-232; RS-422 interface(s)

MORROW DESIGNS, INC.

Morrow Designs, Inc.
600 McCormick St.
San Leandro, CA 94577
(415) 430-1970 Est. 1976

● Morrow Network

Bus ☐ Baseband ☐ CPU: Dynanet Products PC-Bus ☐ Twisted pair cable ☐ 64 connections ☐ 1984 ☐ Pricing — $299

NBI, INC.

NBI, Inc.
3450 Mitchell Lane
Boulder, CO 80301
(303) 444-5710 Est. 1973

● NBI Net

Bus ☐ Baseband ☐ Contention (CSMA/CD) ☐ CPU: NBI System One IWS ☐ Several hundred connections ☐ 10M bps max. ☐ 1983 ☐ Pricing — $900/connection

NCR CORP.

NCR Corp.
1700 S. Patterson Blvd.
Dayton, OH 45479
(513) 445-2380 Est. 1884

● Mirlan

Bus ☐ Baseband ☐ Contention (CSMA/CD) ☐ Central controller required ☐ CPU: NCR POS devices ☐ 1M bps max. ☐ 1983

NESTAR SYSTEMS, INC.

Nestar Systems, Inc.
2585 E. Bayshore Rd.
Palo Alto, CA 94303
(415) 493-2223 Est. 1978

● PLAN 4000

Bus; Starburst; Unconstrained (without loops) ☐ Baseband ☐ Token passing (statistical polling) ☐ CPU: Apple LISA, II, III using

BASIC, Apple Pascal, CP/M, DOS, SOS; IBM PCDOS, UCSD p-system ☐ Coaxial cable ☐ 255 connections ☐ 2.5M bps max. ☐ 4 miles between workstations max. distance ☐ File transfer server; IBM 3270, 3780 Emulators; Telex server gateway(s) ☐ 1982 ☐ Pricing — $595 per network interface card

NETWORK SYSTEMS CORP.

Network Systems Corp.
7600 Boone Ave., N.
Minneapolis, MN 55428
(612) 425-2202 Est. 1974

● HYPERbus

Bus ☐ Baseband ☐ Contention (CSMA/CA) ☐ Coaxial cable; Optical fiber ☐ Unlimited connections ☐ 10M bps max. ☐ 5,000 ft. max. distance ☐ RS-232; 3270; 8 or 16-bit parallel DMA; T1; Satellite interface(s) ☐ 75 installed ☐ 1983 ☐ Pricing — $495-$6,000/connection

● HYPERchannel

Bus ☐ Baseband ☐ Contention (CSMA/CA) ☐ CPU: IBM; CDC; DEC; Honeywell; Burroughs; Cray; Tandem; Harris; DG; Perkin-Elmer; Prime; HP; Gould/SEL; Cray; ICL; Cii/Honeywell Bull; Siemens; Sperry-Univac; Modcomp ☐ Coaxial cable ☐ 256 connections ☐ 50M bps max. ☐ 10,000 ft. between nodes max. distance ☐ Link adapter to carrier facilities (including satellites); Network adapters for CPU/CPU transfer gateway(s) ☐ 2,000 installed ☐ 1977

● PLAN 2000

Bus ☐ Baseband ☐ Token passing (statistical polling) ☐ CPU: IBM PC, XT, PC compatibles ☐ 255 connections ☐ 2.5M bps max. ☐ 22,000 ft. between stations max. distance

● PLAN 3000

Bus ☐ Baseband ☐ Token passing (statistical polling) ☐ CPU: Apple II, III; IBM PC, XT ☐ Coaxial cable ☐ 255 connections ☐ 22,-000 ft. between stations max. distance ☐ File transfer server; Telex server gateway(s)

NORTH STAR COMPUTERS, INC.

North Star Computers, Inc.
14440 Catalina St.
San Leandro, CA 94577
(415) 357-8500 Est. 1976

GUIDE TO LOCAL AREA NETWORKS

● NorthNet

Bus □ Baseband □ Contention (CSMA/PA)
Positive Acknowledgement □ CPU: North
Star Advantage □ Twisted pair cable □ 64
connections □ 880K bps max. □ 10,000 ft.
max. distance □ RS-232 interface(s) □ TWX;
TLX; HPIB device gateway(s) □ 250 installed □ 1983 □ Pricing — $400/connec-
tion

NOVELL, INC.

Novell, Inc.
1170 N. Industrial Park Dr.
Orem, UT 84057
(801) 226-8202 Est. 1983

● NETWARE/S

Star; Linear □ Baseband □ Record/file
locking □ Central controller required □ CPU:
IBM PC; CPM/86; Victor 9000; TI Professional □ Twisted pair cable; Coaxial cable □
24 (Star); 65 (Linear) connections □ 12M
bps max. □ 3,000 ft. from each workstation
to network processor max. distance □ SNA;
Ethernet; Omninet gateway(s) □ 350 installed □ 1982 □ Pricing — $695

● NETWARE/X

Bus □ CPU: IBM PC, XT □ Coaxial cable □
255 connections □ 1.43M bps max. □ 4,000
ft. max. distance

ORCHID TECHNOLOGY, INC.

Orchid Technology, Inc.
47790 Westinghouse Dr.
Fremont, CA 94539
(415) 490-8586 Est. 1982

● PCNET

Bus □ Baseband □ Contention (CSMA/CD)
□ CPU: IBM PC □ Coaxial cable □ 64,000
connections □ 1M bps max. □ 7,000 ft. max.
distance □ 25,000 installed □ 1982 □ Pricing — $1,490 (2 network interface cards, 20
ft. cable, software)

PERCOM DATA CORP.

Percom Data Corp.
11220 Pagemill Rd.
Dallas, TX 75243
(214) 340-5800 Est. 1968

● Percomnet

Addressed Token passing □ Baseband □
Token passing (statistical polling) □ CPU:
IBM PC and compatibles □ Twisted pair
cable □ 254 connections.□ 1M bps max. □
10,000 ft. max. distance □ Ethernet; IBM
3270 gateway(s) □ 500 installed □ 1983 □
Pricing — $595 per node

PRAGMATRONICS, INC.

Pragmatronics, Inc.
2015 10th St.
Boulder, CO 80302
(303) 444-2600 Est. 1979

● TIENET

Bus; Non-rooted tree □ Baseband □ Contention (CSMA/CD) □ CPU: Apple II; Bruker
Aspect 2000; CDC Cyber 750; DEC LSI-11,
PDP-11/10, 34, 44; DG NOVA 4/X; HP 125;
Honeywell 66/80; IBM PC; Onyx C 8002;
Osborne I; Perkin Elmer 3210, 7/16, 32; Radio Shack TRS-80/11; Sanyo S-100 Bus;
Univac 1108 (Exec 8) □ Coaxial cable □ 200
(24,000 stations) connections □ 1M bps
max. □ 5 miles max. distance □ RS-232;
RS-449 interface(s) □ BSC; HDLC gate-
way(s) □ 4 installed □ 1979 □ Pricing —
$700/station average; $626 (400 stations);
$910 (12 stations)

PRIME COMPUTER, INC.

Prime Computer, Inc.
Prime Park MS15-11
Natick, MA 01760
(617) 655-8000 Est. 1972

● RINGNET

Physical ring (addressing) □ Baseband □
Token passing (statistical polling) □ CPU:
Prime 50 Series □ Twinax cable □ 247 connections □ 10M bps max. □ 750 ft. between
nodes max. distance □ RS-232; Prime controller interface(s) □ Part of PRIMENET; provides access to most standard protocols
including X.25 gateway(s) □ 1979 □ Pricing
— $5,000 per PRIMENET Node Controller
(plus PRIMENET software)

PROLINK CORP.

Prolink Corp.
5757 Central Ave.
Boulder, CO 80301
(303) 447-2800 Est. 1980

148

WHAT IS COMMERCIALLY AVAILABLE?

● PROloop

Physical ring (series); Bus; Reconfigurable Ring □ Baseband □ Bidirectional store-and-forward of datagrams of each device □ Central controller required □ CPU: Prolink interconnect devices □ Coaxial cable □ 62 connections □ 10M bps max. □ 350 meters between active nodes max. distance □ RS-232 interface(s) □ BSC; SDLC gateway(s) □ 25 installed □ 1981 □ Pricing — $80/connection (Tap through Loop Access Box)

PROTEON, INC.

Proteon, Inc.
24 Crescent St.
Waltham, MA 02154
(617) 894-1980 Est. 1972

● proNET Star-Shaped Ring

Logical ring; Physical string of stars □ Baseband □ Token passing □ CPU: Vendor provides host specific board for Unibus, Q-Bus, Multibus; IBM PC □ Twisted pair cable; Optical fiber; Coaxial cable; Infrared □ 255 connections □ 10M bps max. □ Node-to-node separation 100 meters (twisted pair); 10 kilometers (fiberoptic) max. distance □ IEEE-488; Terminal Interface Unit for up to 16 RS-232C ports; Unibus; Q-Bus; Multibus; IBM PC (Internal bus) interface(s) □ HDLC; X.25; Arpanet; IBM channel; TCP-IP; DECnet gateway(s) □ 600 installed □ 1981 □ Pricing — $2,550 Ring to Unibus, Q-Bus, Multibus (qty. 25 up); $595 (IBM PC)

RACAL-MILGO

Racal-Milgo
(subsidiary of Racal Electronics, Ltd.)
8600 Northwest 41st St.
Miami, FL 33166
(305) 592-8600 Est. 1955

● Planet

Ring □ Baseband □ Token passing (statistical polling) □ Central controller required □ CPU: Z80 based □ Coaxial cable □ 500 connections □ 10M bps max. □ Up to 950 ft. between TAPs max. distance □ RS-232 interface(s) □ 100 installed □ 1981 □ Pricing — $800 (medium-size systems)

SCIENTIFIC DATA SYSTEMS, INC.

Scientific Data Systems, Inc.
344 Main St.
Venice, CA 90291
(213) 390-8673 Est. 1977

● SDSNET

Branching non-rooted tree □ Baseband □ Contention (CSMA/CD) □ CPU: SDS □ Coaxial cable □ 255 connections □ 1M bps max. □ 1,000 meters max. distance □ 1981 □ Pricing — $5,400 per station

SD SYSTEMS, INC.

SD Systems Inc.
(subsidiary of Syntech Intl., Ltd.)
10111 Miller Rd.
Dallas, TX 75238
(214) 340-0303 Est. 1977

● MARS/Net

Bus; Physical ring (addressing) □ Baseband □ Contention (CSMA/CD) □ Central controller required □ CPU: Any S-100 Bus or Multibus running CP/M or MP/M □ Twisted pair cable □ 256 connections □ 800K bps max. □ 3,000 ft. max. distance □ RS-232 interface(s) □ 1981 □ Pricing — $500 per node interface

SIECOR CORP.

Siecor Corp.
489 Siecor Pike
Hickory, NC 28603
(704) 328-2171 Est. 1980

● Fiberlan-Net 10

Bus; Star □ Baseband □ Contention (CSMA/CD) □ Optical fiber □ Up to 4,000 connections □ 10M bps max. □ 2.5 kilometers max. distance □ IEEE-488; RS-232 interface(s) □ Ethernet gateway(s) □ 3 installed □ 1983

SPACE COAST SYSTEMS, INC.

Space Coast Systems, Inc.
301 S. Washington Ave.
Titusville, FL 32796
(305) 268-0872 Est. 1983

● PC-LINK

Star □ Central controller required □ 64 connections □ 100 ft. max. distance □ 1984 □ Pricing — $370

149

STANDARD DATA CORP.

Standard Data Corp.
1500 Northwest 62nd St., Suite 508
Ft. Lauderdale, FL 33309
(305) 776-7177   Est. 1979

● Disc-less Network

Bus □ Baseband; Optional broadband □
Contention (CSMA/CD) □ CPU: IBM PC, XT;
Z-100; IBM PC compatibles □ Coaxial cable; Optional fiberoptic □ 255 connections □
3M bps max. □ 1 kilometer; Optional broadband 75 kilometers max. distance □ IEEE-488; RS-232; S-100 Bus; Multibus; DEC
Unibus; VERSAbus interface(s) □ X.25;
Ethernet gateway(s) □ 200 installed □ 1983
□ Pricing — $695

STARNET DATA SYSTEMS

Starnet Data Systems
(subsidiary of Protex Industries, Inc.)
1331 W. Evans Ave.
Denver, CO 80223
(303) 935-3566   Est. 1921

● Starnet II

Star □ Baseband □ User-command to data
stream □ CPU: 8085 □ Twisted pair cable;
Coaxial cable □ 4,096 connections □ 19.2K
bps max. □ 400 ft. max. distance □ IEEE-488; RS-232; RS-449; A-D; D-A; Dataproducts; Centronics; Current loop; TTL interface(s) □ 7 installed □ 1981 □ Pricing —
$1,000/connection

STEARNS COMPUTER SYSTEMS

Stearns Computer Systems
10901 Bren Rd., E., P.O. Box 9384
Minneapolis, MN 55440
(612) 936-2000   Est. 1982

● MICRONETWORK

Star □ Baseband □ Central controller required □ CPU: 8086 □ Twisted pair cable □
5 connections □ 19.2K bps max. □ 3,000 ft.
max. distance □ RS-232 interface(s) □ 25
installed □ 1984 □ Pricing — $500

STRATUS COMPUTER, INC.

Stratus Computer, Inc.
17 Strathmore Rd.
Natick, MA 01760
(617) 653-1466   Est. 1980

● StrataLink

Physical ring (addressing) □ Baseband □
Data sense multiple access/collision detect
□ CPU: Stratus/32 □ Coaxial cable □ 255
connections □ 12.5M bps max. □ 25 miles
circumference max. distance □ Vendor specific interface(s) □ HDLC; SDLC; BSC gateway(s) □ 1982 □ Pricing — $5,000 per
system

SYDIS, INC.

Sydis, Inc.
410 E. Plumeria Dr.
San Jose, CA 95134
(408) 945-1100   Est. 1982

● SYLINK

Star □ Baseband □ Contention (CSMA/CD)
□ Central controller required □ CPU: Sydis,
Inc. □ Twisted pair cable □ 200 connections
□ 320K bps max. □ 4,000 ft. max. distance
□ RS-232 interface(s) □ BSC; SDLC; HDLC;
SNA; X.25 gateway(s) □ 1984

SYTEK, INC.

Sytek, Inc.
1225 Charleston Rd.
Mountain View, CA 94043
(415) 966-7300   Est. 1979

● LocalNet

Bus □ Broadband □ Contention (CSMA/
CD); FDM; Packet switching □ CPU: Z80 □
Coaxial cable □ 24,000 connections □ 1.5M
bps max. □ 50 kilometer radius max. distance □ RS-232; Unibus interface(s) □ X.25;
BSC; Ethernet gateway(s) □ 350 installed □
1981 □ Pricing — $345-$545/connection

TECMAR, INC.

Tecmar, Inc.
6225 Cochran Rd.
Solon, OH 44139
(216) 349-0600   Est. 1974

● ComNet

Bus; Physical ring (addressing) □ Broadband □ Contention (CSMA/CD) □ CPU: IBM
PC □ Coaxial cable □ 10M bps max. □ 1983
□ Pricing — $1,695-$3,295 per station

TRANTOR SYSTEMS, LTD.

Trantor Systems, Ltd.
4432 Enterprise St., Suite I
Fremont, CA 94538
(415) 490-3441   Est. 1982

WHAT IS COMMERCIALLY AVAILABLE?

• The Web

Star □ Token passing (statistical polling) □ Central controller required □ CPU: Osborne; Apple; CP/M □ Twisted pair cable; Ribbon cable □ 8 connections □ 25K bps max. □ 50 ft. max. distance □ RS-232; SASI interface(s) □ BSC; SDLC; HDLC gateway(s) □ 10 installed □ 1983 □ Pricing — $1,995 (4 workstations)

UNGERMANN-BASS, INC.

Ungermann-Bass, Inc.
2560 Mission College Blvd.
Santa Clara, CA 95050
(408) 496-0111 Est. 1979

• Net/One

Bus □ Baseband; Broadband □ CSMA, broadband; Contention (CSMA/CD), baseband □ CPU: Ungermann-Bass Network Interface Unit (NIU) provides transparency for most standard devices □ Coaxial cable; Optical fiber □ 2,400 per network segment baseband; 36,000 broadband connections □ 10M bps baseband; 5M bps broadband; 10M bps fiber optics max. □ 2,500 meters per network baseband; 10 miles broadband; 2,800 meters per network fiber optic max. distance □ IEEE-488; RS-232; RS-449; 8, 16, 32-bit parallel; DEC DR11-W/B interface(s) □ Ethernet; V.35 gateway(s) □ 400 installed □ 1980 □ Pricing — $500

VECTOR GRAPHIC, INC.

Vector Graphic, Inc.
500 N. Ventura Park Rd.
Thousand Oaks, CA 91320
(805) 499-5831 Est. 1976

• LINC

Physical ring (addressing) □ Baseband □ Token passing (statistical polling) □ CPU: Vector 4 microcomputers □ Twisted pair cable □ 16 connections □ 750K bps max. □ 2 miles max. distance □ RS-422 interface(s) □ SDLC gateway(s) □ 1982 □ Pricing — $695/connection

WANG LABORATORIES, INC.

Wang Laboratories. Inc.
1 Industrial Ave., MS 1307B
Lowell, MA 01851
(617) 459-5000 Est. 1951

• WangNet

Bus; Physical ring (addressing); Loop; XMT and REC busses □ Broadband □ Contention (CSMA/CD); FDM (64-ch.) □ CPU: WangNet Interface hardware for connection of most standard devices □ Coaxial cable □ 62,535 connections □ 12M bps max. □ Over 4 miles max. distance □ RS-232; Cable interface unit; RS-449 interface(s) □ Wang Data Switch; Remote microwave; Satellite gateway(s) □ Pricing — $7,500 Technical Control and Management Monitor System

WESTERN DIGITAL CORP.

Western Digital Corp.
2445 McCabe Way
Irvine, CA 92714
(714) 557-3550 Est. 1970

• NetSource/PC-LAN

Logical ring □ Token passing (statistical polling) □ Central controller required □ CPU: IBM PC □ 254 connections □ 1M bps max. □ 10,000 ft. max. distance □ 1984

WINSOURCE, INC.

Winsource, Inc.
5 Northway Lane, N.
Latham, NY 12110
(518) 783-1336 Est. 1982

• Winnet

Star □ Baseband □ Contention (CSMA/CD) □ Central controller required □ CPU: Winsource □ Twisted pair cable □ 32 data; 400 voice connections □ 9,600 bps max. □ 1,-000 ft. max. distance □ RS-232 interface(s) □ 35 installed □ 1982 □ Pricing — $200/connection

XCOMP, INC.

Xcomp, Inc.
3554 Ruffin Rd., S.
San Diego, CA 92123
(619) 573-0077 Est. 1977

• X-Net

Bus □ Baseband □ CPU: IBM PC □ 255 connections □ Pricing — $490

GUIDE TO LOCAL AREA NETWORKS

XEROX CORP.

Xerox Corp.
800 Long Ridge Rd., P.O. Box 1600
Stanford, CT. 06904
(203) 329-8700 Est. 1906

● Ethernet

Bus; Physical ring (addressing) ☐ Baseband ☐ Contention (CSMA/CD) ☐ Coaxial cable ☐ 1,024 connections ☐ 10M bps max. ☐ 1.5 miles max. distance ☐ RS-232 interface(s) ☐ 500 installed ☐ 1980 ☐ Pricing — $750 max. (depends on equipment type)

XYPLEX, INC.

Xyplex, Inc.
100 Domino Dr.
Concord, MA 01742
(617) 317-1400 Est. 1981

● The XYPLEX System

Bus ☐ Broadband ☐ Contention (CSMA/CD) ☐ Coaxial cable ☐ 255 connections ☐ 1M bps max. ☐ 6 miles max. distance ☐ RS-232; DEC Unibus interface(s) ☐ 25 installed ☐ 1982 ☐ Pricing — $750/connection

15

WHAT DOES IBM HAVE TO OFFER?

Considering the strength of IBM's influence on the computer market, it is only natural to wonder about the company's networking products and future intentions. For the past few years, IBM has been tantalizing the industry with promises of a token-passing ring network designed to tie together all IBM products. In keeping with new IBM tradition, though, little has actually been said about the product, and there are more rumors than facts. There is little doubt, however, that this long awaited network will come to pass; the only question is when. Speculation within the industry places its arrival about mid-1985 or early 1986.

In the meanwhile, IBM has released a local area network for its smaller personal computer products. Designated the IBM PC Network, it is a low-cost, broadband network designed to link together IBM's line of personal computers. The IBM PC Network is compatible with all IBM personal computers including the IBM PC, IBM XT, *Portable* PC, and the newest release, the IBM Personal Computer AT. It is not, however, compatible with the IBM PC*jr*.

ABOUT THE NETWORK

The IBM PC Network is a broadband local area network that uses single-channel frequency translation. If you've already read Chapter 10, then you know that it is similar to the broadband networks offered by Wang and Sytek. The network takes the output signal from the network nodes and uses it to modulate an RF signal.

There are some differences, though. For one, IBM has opted to use a single-channel converter for its PC Network rather than the multi-channel networks offered by Wang or Sytek. IBM's rationale for this seemingly limited choice was to offer the IBM user low-cost entry into the world of networking. IBM did, however, choose to go with the more expensive frequency-conversion technique pioneered by Systek rather than use the dual-cable setup exploited by Wang. In fact, Sytek has been selected to be the OEM (original equipment manufacturer) for this portion of the system.

IBM PC TRANSLATOR

The frequency conversion is handled by an IBM PC Translator Unit, designed and built by Sytek, and each network must have one. The translator accepts modem-driven messages from the network nodes at an input frequency of 50.75 MHz and converts them to 219.00 MHz. The messages are then retransmitted over the network at the higher frequency. Consequently, all network

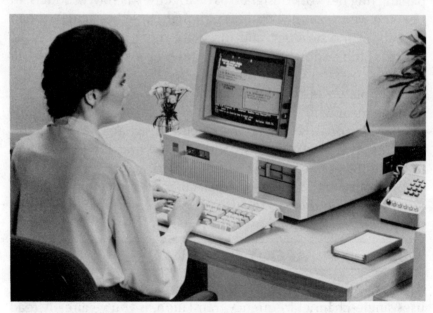

Along with the release of the IBM PC AT, IBM shocked the computer industry with the announcement of the IBM PC Network. Basically, the PC Network is a broadband, CSMA/CD network that incorporates a single-channel Sytek frequency converter. The release of the IBM PC Network is likely to have the same impact on the industry as the introduction of the IBM Personal Computer—enormous.

nodes must listen to the upper band to intercept messages and data.

The Translator Unit consists of a single printed circuit board housed in a rigid metal cabinet. The unit is powered by an outboard power supply that plugs into a standard electrical outlet. Sytek, in accordance with IBM specifications, has designed the Translator Unit for reliability and minimal servicing. To be exact, there are no field adjustments made to the translator itself, and the unit can be hidden in an out-of-the-way place with no worry. Once installed, it can be forgotten.

CONNECTING THE NETWORK

The IBM Translator Unit can support up to eight IBM personal computers on its own, and each computer can be located up to 200 feet away from the Translator Unit. The Translator Unit connects to the networking nodes using 75-ohm coax cable. In fact, the network uses the same cable found in many CATV installations. This cable is inexpensive, readily available, and easy to install. IBM has even gone so far as to specify the ever popular F-type connector for the cable termination. In case you don't know what an F connector is, just look at the back of your TV set and you will see one. You can buy them almost anywhere, including Radio Shack.

But the network is not limited to the eight nodes supported by the Translator Unit. It is expandable to 72 nodes. In order to network more than eight computers, though, you must use one or more of the IBM extension kits. Altogether, IBM offers three network extension kits: short, medium, and long. First, however, you need a Base Expander. The Base Expander is a splitter, of sorts, that plugs into the Translator's expansion port and allows you to connect up to eight expansion kits to the Translator Unit.

Each expansion kit also permits up to eight nodes to be connected to it, for a total of 64. When added to the original eight ports, the figure totals 72 nodes. Each expansion kit is tailored specifically for the network and the distance involved, and they are not interchangeable.

The Short-Distance Kit, for instance, connects directly to the network Base Expander and supports the attachment of up to eight additional IBM personal computers at a distance of 200 feet. In actuality, the expansion kit itself is nothing more than a splitter with a 20-db insertion pad. It connects the Base Expander through a one-foot length of cable, and permits up to 200 feet of extension from it to the networking nodes.

Because the signal is so intense at this point, the 20-db attenuation pad is needed to keep the signal from swamping the input of the splitter and rendering the data unusable. Likewise, an 8-db attenuator is placed in line with the Medium-Distance Kit.

The Medium-Distance Kit allows the Base Expander to connect to the Translator Unit and the Medium-Distance Kit divider unit. In addition to that, an extra 200 feet of cable is allowed from the extension kit's divider module to the node itself, for a total radius of 600 feet. Like the Short-Distance Kit, it will support eight additional nodes.

The Long-Distance Kit extends the network's working distance to 1000 feet. An extension of 800 feet is permissible between the Base Expander and the extension kit; when this is added to the 200 feet between the extension splitter and the node, the total radius becomes 1000 feet. In this instance, however, no attenuation pad has to be inserted in the line; the losses incurred by the coax cable are enough to keep the network signal voltage within limits.

It must be noted, however, that the kits do not come with coax cable, except for the one-foot link supplied with the Short-Distance Kit. Connecting cables are purchased separately in lengths ranging from 25 to 200 feet. As previously mentioned, the coax is of the garden variety, typically RG-11 or RG-6, and doesn't have to be purchased from IBM.

By using readily available CATV cable and limiting the size of the expansion kits, IBM has achieved a network that is low in cost yet versatile enough to meet virtually all future needs. You can expand your network at any time in cost-effective increments.

Moreover, the network is not even limited to one channel. By purchasing commercially available translator units, you can expand your network to almost limitless proportions. A simple Sytek six-channel frequency converter can easily explode the network to accommodate upwards of 20,000 nodes with no modification whatsoever to cable installation.

NETWORK CONFIGURATION

The way you connect the nodes together with the coax constitutes the network configuration. Basically, the network can be put into two configurations. Using your knowledge of network topology, though, you will probably recognize them as one and the same.

The network is basically configured as a rooted tree with the Translator Unit serving as the focal point. All network messages are funneled into the translator, frequency converted, and redistributed over the network. This, of course, is only a rough analysis of the real situation, because you can modify the network topology to meet your specific needs.

The star toplogy is the simplest network to design and install. The star begins with the Translation Unit itself. Radiating from its outputs can be eight nodes—all at distances up to 200 feet. The resulting topology is that of a star because each node must feed the centrally located Translator Unit and have the message frequency converted for retransmission. In a sense, the network is sequential when sending a message—because it has to pass through the Translator Unit—but becomes broadcast when the message is converted and placed back on the network. (If all this sounds confusing, review Chapter 4).

IBM PC star networks are straightforward and to the point. Little signal is lost between the Translator Unit and a node—the only loss being what the cable itself absorbs. This type of network is also easily installed and expandable, as each node simply runs a new cable to the Translator Unit or extension kit hub. The star topology's main trade-off is that implementing it requires large amounts of cable and it doesn't adapt well to certain enviroments.

The alternative is the bus configuration. When the physical design suggests the bus topology, the materials cost may be lower than the star topology. The bus topology has a slightly different design approach from the star and requires only one main feeder cable to the Translator Unit.

The main bus cable is routed through the LAN area, and nodes are attached to it using directional cable taps. Every tap made to the bus, however, reduces the total amount of available signal.

Let's take an example. For the sake of argument, let's say that you start off with a signal strength of 4 and add one tap to the network. This tap will bleed off one unit of power and leave the network with a signal strength of 3. Likewise, two taps absorb 2 units and leave 2. Four taps will use up all the available signal. In effect, that is the limit to the size of your network. Of course, the IBM PC Network can support many more than four nodes.

Of more consequence, however, is insertion loss. Basically, insertion loss is the amount of signal lost when a mechanical connection is made to the cable. As a rule of thumb, expect about 3 db of insertion loss for each connector. One way of minimizing insertion loss is to connect more than one node to a tap, in much the same way as a lamp extension cord allows the connection of up to three outlets. The resulting topology is that of a rooted tree.

Tree topology allows the functional separation of responsibilities while minimizing insertion loss. The branch divides the signal power among the feeder cables, and the feeder cables distribute that power to the nodes. For example, picture a two-way splitter that branches into two bus feeder lines. The feeder lines can then each be split to connect to the individual nodes. The branching-tree topology is a logical extension of the bus design. The advantage of a tree network is that it continues to operate even when one or more of the nodes or braches are not active.

NETWORK INTERFACE

The IBM PC Network operates at 2MHz under the guidance of an Intel 80188 microprocessor. Since the network is passive in nature, each node must have one of these microprocessors in order to participate in network operations.

The processor chip comes aboard a Network Adapter Card that plugs into an expansion slot inside the computer. The Adapter Card includes nine feet of attachment cord that can be connected directly to the Translator Unit or to an IBM network expansion kit. Of course, the cards are purchased separately for each machine, thus further emphasizing IBM's commitment to modularity.

Each card include 16K of RAM memory and a BIOS (Basic Input/Output System) chip. The BIOS chip contains a translator program that puts the unique features of the local area network into standard format and makes its operation transparent to the user. In other words, the user merely has to issue a couple of simple commands, and the BIOS program takes it from there. It will log onto the network, transmit your message, and receive an acknowledgement with no further action on your part. It can even recognize data collision and retransmit your message if a collision occurs.

The BIOS program even allows you to use real names, rather than code names, when addressing other nodes. Simple real-world names such as Bob and Jane are totally acceptable and much easier to relate to than QWP-002. Other network commands include CALL and LISTEN.

The adapter board carries out all operations using Carrier-Sense, Multiple-Access/with Collision Detection (CSMA/CD) protocol. As a matter of fact, the Network Adapter Card uses an Ethernet-compatible 82586 communications chip for the network interface.

NETWORK MESSAGES

The IBM PC Network communicates in two different modes. After the names for each of the network nodes have been specified, two of them can communicate with each other in a mode called a *session*. The session is very similar to a telecommunication connection, with its point-to-point, full duplex operation that is not unlike the way telephones are connected. In the IBM PC Network, the session is often referred to as a virtual circuit. Once the session is established, the transfer of data through the network can begin.

Session messages are set up in a session table using the CALL and LISTEN commands. Once the session is established, it can be called on the screen at any time using the abbreviation. In other words, it's like filing a program away in a file name and retrieving it using a simple name. Once a session is recalled, a virtual bidirectional link is established between the two parties with no further intervention on their part. Up to 32 different session connections may be stored in this manner.

The IBM network also supports messages called datagrams. Datagrams differ from the virtual circuit connection in that control of the network becomes the responsibility of the user, and operations are less transparent. Datagram service does not provide point-to-point connection and is used to send data to either a single or group name, or to broadcast a general message to everyone. Datagram support differs from session support in several ways.

To begin with, messages sent via datagram are never acknowledged by the receiver's adapter, so it is up to the parties involved to establish their own form of acknowledgment. Messages are also limited in length to 512 bytes. Session messages, on the other hand, can send over over 8000 bytes within a single frame. Given its general broadcast ability, though, you will find datagram service quite useful.

IBM PC NETWORK SPECIFICATIONS

IBM PC Network Adapter
Maximum data rate: 2 Mbits per second
CSMA/CD access protocol
Maximum distance to Network Translator: 16,500 feet
Maximum IBM PC nodes: 1,000
Transmit frequency: 50.75 MHz
Receive frequency: 219.00 MHz
Channel bandwidth: 6 MHz each

IBM PC Network Translator Unit
Maximum attachments: 256
Input frequency: 50.75 MHz
Output frequency: 219.00 MHz
Channel offset: 168.25 MHz
Translator bandwidth: 6 MHz
Translator gain: 36dB

IBM PC Network Cabling Components
75 ohm coaxial cabling
Standard F connector terminations
Maximum IBM PC nodes: 72
Maximum radius: 1,000 feet
Attenuation, forward path: 41.75dB (to any node)
Attenuation, reverse path: 41.75dB (to any node)
Crosstalk isolation: 18dB minimum (to any node)

WHAT CAN I EXPECT FOR THE FUTURE?

ESSAYS BY:

Bob Davi
Orchid Technology

Ralph Ungermann
Ungermann-Bass

Jim Nichols
Futurex Security Systems

Bruce Richardson
Wang Laboratories

Ralph Ungermann
President, Ungermann-Bass, Inc.

Ralph Ungermann is President of Ungermann-Bass, Inc., a data communications manufacturing and marketing firm. He is credited with many innovations in the Local Area Network field and the holder of several patents.

FUTURE TRENDS IN LOCAL AREA NETWORKING

YEAR OF THE LAN

It is apparent that there is an ongoing proliferation of powerful distributed information processing equipment at continually declining costs and increasing performance. Allowing these distributed processing devices from various vendors to exchange information at high speeds and to share expensive resources is a critical task that is complicated by different physical interfaces and incompatible protocols and languages. Unprecedented increased use of both personal computers and powerful workstations is now creating a huge demand for high-performance local area networks (LANs). Therefore, I see this as the year when local area networks will become the critical element of installations of any significant size.

Until recently, most installations consisted of large numbers of terminals connected to time-shared processors, with terminal interconnect achieved through point-to-point wiring, or digital PBXs. LANs provide an improved ability to interconnect terminals to processors, but were actually developed to provide effective

162

distributed processing. Effective distributed processing, however, requires radically different communications technology than that required for simple terminal switching. For example, LANs are unique in their use of a very high-speed, shared communications medium. This technology permits a single device to use the entire available bandwidth of the system for the short duration of its transmission—ranging from one to 50 million bits per second (Mbps). This speed is essential to enable large files to be moved between workstations and centralized data bases very rapidly to maintain user productivity. The sharing of the media allows instantaneous access to all devices on the network. This technology contrasts with the conventional PBX or data switch approach of dividing bandwidth simultaneously among many slower transmissions. In addition, LANs use distributed communications processors, rather than centralized processors, providing the dedicated intelligence needed to interconnect specific devices and to maximize reliability. For the next few years LANs will continue to coexist with PBXs because they provide effective solutions to quite different problems, although true voice and data intelligence will eventually occur.

MARKET SEGMENTATION

The local area network market is divided into three distinct segments. These are largely non-overlapping, and in fact, are often more complementary than they are competitive. In one market LANs are used as "proprietary" integral parts of computer systems, and have been optimized to sell their own brand of information processing equipment.

The second segment of the LAN market I refer to is "special purpose." This segment includes local area networks that have been designed and optimized to network together specific types of devices such as mainframe computers and personal computers.

The third market segment is the one that Ungermann-Bass set out to create in 1979—the one which we call "general purpose." Within this segment LANs are optimized for flexibility. The goal is to provide the capability to interconnect devices ranging from mainframes to personal computers to robots, regardless of brand;

in the factory, the office or the laboratory; across the country, or around the world. I estimate that the size of the general-purpose LAN market will exceed $120 million in 1984, and should at least double annually for several years. This means that the market may well be in excess of $1 billion by 1987.

INDUSTRY STANDARDS

In the future, it will be essential that the general-purpose LANs use worldwide industry standards such as Ethernet. A new technology called token-passing is rapidly emerging mainly due to IBM's support. When IBM officially announces systems using its proprietary LANs, the technology utilized will quickly become the most important worldwide standard.

As the LAN market evolves, industry groups such as the European Computer Manufacturer's Association (ECMA) and the Institute of Electrical and Electronic Engineers (IEEE) will continue to define standards for use in the LAN environment. The development of such standards significantly lowers the cost of LAN products due to industry-wide semiconductor implementation and provides the basis for increased compatibility with other vendors' products. Customers need to know that a network installation is a long-term, viable solution to their distributed information-processing requirements.

LAN MEDIA

There are a number of important LAN communications media around which standards will be developed. Successful LAN vendors will need to support the full range of the leading LAN media: broadcast (multiple channel), and baseband (single channel), coaxial cable, and optical fiber. A relatively new network technology, data-grade twisted pair, will gain acceptance quickly because of IBM's support.

The major growth in the near future, however, will be in broadband, which will become more widely used than baseband. By the end of 1984, I think that at least 50 percent of the LANs being installed will use broadband. Optical fiber will continue to be a specialty product for the next two or three years, but will ultimately become a very important medium because of increasing demand for greater bandwidth.

Today LANs for PC clusters operate at speeds of approximately one Mbps, while speeds of general-purpose LANs range from five to ten Mbps and mainframe LANs operate at speeds from 50 to 200 Mbps. As companies network more and more high-performance devices, they will require greater bandwidth in all LAN communications media. The availability of high-speed LANs will allow greater use of centralized databases and distributed intelligence.

INTEGRATED SYSTEMS

The optimum LAN is one which ensures the coexistence of any industry standard communications media. Each medium offers different features and can complement the others. Using this mixed media approach, customers can obtain the most cost-effective, technically sound solution to their organization-wide communications problems. An organization needs a single, well-managed cohesive communications system that can meet both present and future requirements. Effective network management facilities—the ability to configure, control, monitor, and diagnose the LAN system—will be the key to successful system integration.

In summary, I think you will see LANs widely used to implement effective distributed information processing in the very near future. The successful LANs will utilize multiple industry standard communications media support by extensive network management. Most importantly, users will be free to select any vendor's information processing equipment based on capability rather than compatibility.

Bruce Richardson
**Product Marketing Manager,
Wang**

Bruce Richardson is the Product Marketing Manager for Wang's local area network product line. Prior to joining Wang
in 1983, he was director of marketing for a
market research and consulting firm.
Bruce is an MBA candidate at Boston University and holds a BA from Boston
College.

EIGHT MEGATRENDS IN BROADBAND LOCAL NETWORKS

A few years ago the cry heard down the corridors of business
was "Broadband Networks Are Coming! Broadband Networks
Are Coming!"

They're here.

Broadband is no longer the exclusive province of Fortune 100
companies or large universities with scores of buildings. Recent
announcements of inexpensive, user-installable products have
taken a lot of the mystery and risk out of networks. This trend,
coupled with lower rf modem and cable component costs have
made broadband a viable alternative to baseband and twisted
pair.

Surveys show that local networks are being installed in many
diverse environments including multinationals, banks, financial
institutions, government agencies, universities, law firms, airports,
museums, hospitals, and even aircraft carriers.

Chances are very good that your company has installed
broadband or will consider it this year. With that decision behind
you, it's time to set the dial on the Time Machine ahead into the
future. The following represents one view of the *Eight Megatrends*
that will occur over the next several years.

WHAT CAN I EXPECT FOR THE FUTURE?

NEW CORPORATE PHILOSOPHY

1. *The Network as a Corporate Asset*
The network will come to be valued as an integral portion of a corporation's information management strategy. It will no longer be viewed as a standalone technology. PC networks, which sprang up as a means to share resources among multiple workstations, will begin to fade away in favor of a more functional, *systems-based corporate network*. Twisted pair and baseband will not have the power to function in this new environment.

COMMUNICATIONS AS THE LINK BETWEEN DATA PROCESSING AND OFFICE AUTOMATION

2. *Increased Coexistence*
Information processing and distribution have traditionally been divided into three segregated functions—voice communications, data processing, and office automation. These functions have developed separately, resulting in fragmented solutions with different networks for each.

The watchword is co-existence. Vendors will offer integrated solutions which address all three functions. Joint development or alliances between vendors of the various technologies will ensure that the user gets an operational, fully functional solution.

In keeping with the reality of multi-vendor environments, new products and solutions must conform to recognized standards— those developed by national and international committees and those brought forth by dominant vendors (*de facto* standards).

The days of top to bottom universal standards are not yet here. There are almost as many standards committees and de facto standards as there are communication technologies. Standards that evolve gradually will have to be implemented gradually and provide transitions and migrations from installed equipment.

3. *The LAN as the Catalyst to "Global Area Networking"*
At a 1983 conference on local networks, a comment was made that "in two years, discussions of local networks will be passe. The focus will shift from talk of media, topologies, and

access methods, to which vendor can most meet my total networking needs. What we are really talking about is "global area networking."

Customers are beginning to demand complete end-to-end solutions. The local network will serve as the central point for tying together remote sites to the corporate headquarter's computing and data resources. It will provide "transparent" gateways to remote networks at other sites. Users will only need to be concerned with what needs to be communicated, not how the information actually is transmitted.

The local network will provide the impetus for global networking. When local resources are efficiently shared, access to remote data and access by remote users becomes even more desirable. No longer does each desk require its own modem. The advantages of electronic mail can be expanded to worldwide operations.

4. *Integration with the PBX*

The PBX vs. LAN debate has begun to abate as users realize that it is not really an "either/or" issue—the two are complementary rather than competitive technologies. The real question is how do users on one network communicate with users on another.

This is being addressed by both communications and computer vendors in the form of specifications defining the interface beetween processors and PBXs. Within two years PBX users will tie into LAN users via dedicated T1 channels which will tie "information archipelagos" together. Ultimately, users will have a total integration independent of the media or switching system used.

APPLICATIONS

5. *Network Applications*

Over the next few years discussions of networks will certainly focus less on hardware and more on applications. The goal will be to provide easy access to needed information and the means to distribute critical data. Among the applications being introduced now are the following:

WHAT CAN I EXPECT FOR THE FUTURE?

Time Management Services enable users to create and maintain personal calendars and reminder lists and send meeting invitations to other users.

Directory Services support office mail, time management, and file management functions (i.e., name searches, distribution lists, and information access control).

Mail and Messaging Services allow users to exchange packages containing documents, messages, and files. In the future users will be able to pass MS-DOS files, voice, and image documents through the network.

PERFORMANCE

6. *Comprehensive Network Management*

To many users, installing a network without a comprehensive network management and control system is a constant game of "You Bet Your Job." The following represents some of the market requirements that are being generated to meet the mandate of minimal downtime:

Ability to centrally monitor all components both locally and remotely, and provide information on traffic levels, network performance, and quality of service.

Immediate access to information about the location, status and performance of every system on the network, including the name and telephone number of the individual responsible for the equipment.

Automatic notification of the operator in the event of a failure, as well as help in locating and isolating the cause of the problem.

Ability to log operational problems as they occur and print historical reports of network functions.

A modular design that enables the network to tailor the control and management system to specific network requirements.

TECHNOLOGICAL EVOLUTION

7. *Lower Costs, Increased Flexibility, Higher Throughput*

Studies by one market research firm indicate that broadband costs (interface units, cable components) are expected to drop about 50 percent over the next few years. Accelerating the trend towards less expensive networks are the recent announcements of several modular, user-installable networks. These pre-configured products are priced about 40 percent less than the traditional custom-designed networks.

There is a shift from a total broadband implementation to a more flexible approach that allows the incorporation of other media into the network. For example, bridges are being built that allow baseband PC networks to be linked into the corporate network. Fiber optics is being added as component prices drop.

While the highest speed used in office networks today is generally about 10 Million bits per second (Mbps), research is underway on speeds of up to 300 Million bits per second range.

Is that horsepower necessary? It depends on the application. Certainly not if one is sending an electronic message to a colleague concerning lunch plans. Some users will want the increased speed for sending complex graphics or integrated text, data, image, and voice files. Others will want to be able to manipulate digital data from a satellite down link at the speed it is being transmitted.

(Note: We now have 1 MIPS computers with hundreds of millions of bytes of storage on top of our desks. It wasn't so long ago that machines of this class were found only in computer centers.)

INDUSTRY DEVELOPMENTS

8. *Acceptance of Networks as a Present Necessity, Not a "Future"*

Over the next four years, it is estimated that the total number of office networks will grow from 16,000 to 100,000. Architecture Technology Corp. predicts LANs will be $1.5 billion business by 1988.

170

WHAT CAN I EXPECT FOR THE FUTURE?

How do we get there from here? One of the most important developments has been in the area of network standards—one advantage of broadband is that its ample bandwidth enables users to have multiple channels conforming to standards (e.g., 802.3 and 802.4) on the same cable.

Network standards are beginning to assume the role that de facto operating systems have had in the PC marketplace. As demand for standard products increases, there will likely be hundreds of suppliers competing to develop hardware and software for this marketplace. The net result will be more network applications, lower costs, and greater utility.

In the future there will be fewer companies providing LAN alternatives. As users begin to plan for future needs, their analysis will focus not only on the technology, but on the vendor size, support structure, turnkey implementation, and most importantly the products and applications that work across the network. After all, that piece of cable is no longer just 400 MHz of 75-ohm cable. It's a corporate asset.

Jim Nichols
Vice-President, Futurex Security

Jim Nichols is Vice President of Marketing for Futurex Security Systems, a data security and communications manufacturing and marketing firm. Prior to his appointment in July 1984, Mr. Nichols was Executive Director of Jones Futura Foundation, the parent company. Mr. Nichols also holds the concurrent position of Vice President, Technology, of Jones International, Ltd.

ENCRYPTION IN LANs

Encryption is a general term that refers to processing data to secure the information from access or tampering and is specifically used for communication security, stored data security and authentication.

Probably the biggest impact that encryption will have on Local Area Networks is to allow them to be used in areas where they otherwise would not be allowed because of access control and security requirements. Encryption will be used to secure communications, secure storage, and perhaps most importantly authentication.

Communication security includes point-to-point encryption on the network, encryption between the network and host, or encryption between networks, and may take the form of session security between points or aggregate security.

File Security

File security takes two forms: one is Private File Security and the other is Aggregate File Security to a network storage device.

Private File Security allows an individual at an access point to store information on a network public device. The individual specifies how data is to be stored, and the private encryption key under which the data is encrypted and stored. To retrieve the data the individual specifies the data to be recovered and the encryption key.

Aggregate File Security provides encrypted storage of all data sent to a public storage device from an access point. The key belongs to the device and is invoked automatically when data is stored or retrieved.

Authentication

Authentication takes several forms: authentication of devices; authentication of users; authentication of software; and authentication of data. Encryption is at the heart of authentication; data is passed through an authentication algorithm which uses the cryptographic process to generate an authentication code that can only be created if the encryption key is known. The most common form in use today is MAC (Message Authentication Code). Here the message (data) is passed through the authentication routine and a MAC is generated and appended to the message prior to transmission. At the receiving point, the message is authenticated by passing it through the authentication algorithm using the same key that was used at the point of origin. If the same MAC is generated, it verifies that the message received is identical to the message sent. For audit purposes, the message can be stored with its MAC and authenticated at any time in the future.

For Local Area Networks, authentication will allow other points (host, other networks, and other access points) to authenticate the hardware and/or the individual requesting access to the services. The procedure used will be similar to that used to authenticate messages. Here, coded or encrypted data will be exchanged, decrypted and authenticated to verify that the communicating devices and/or individuals are the intended participants.

After the session is established, the data may or may not be encrypted depending on the sensitivity of the communications. Encryption, in this case, guarantees the security of passwords, key phrases, and the generation and security of unique user authentication codes and session establishment.

Encryption has applications in software authentication: (1) The ability to uniquely couple a software package to a specific piece of hardware, and (2) the ability to determine that the software running in a particular device has not been modified.

In the first instance, software is encrypted using the key known only to the device where the software is to be used. When a program is to be run, the software is loaded into the device and decrypted for execution.

In the second case, the software is stored with a message authentication code appended to the program. (This could include both program and data stored on a public access device.) When the software and data are retrieved from the public storage device, the authentication code is verified to ensure that no change has occurred, either accidentally or intentionally. As with the message authentication code, the software authentication code is developed under a key known only to the authentication device. Encryption, therefore, is merely a tool that can be used in a variety of ways for LAN security. Communication security and storage security are the most widely known; however, in the future, authentication of messages, users, devices, and software have the potential of being the dominant application on such public access networks as LANs. These applications will open the use of LAN technology to a much wider market and a greater variety of users on a given network.

Robert Davi
**Marketing Director,
Orchid Technology**

Bob Davi is Director of Marketing at
Orchid Technology, a Fremont, CA based
technology company. Orchid was among
the first enterpreneurial firms to offer
Local Area Networks for use with the personal computer.

WHERE IS NETWORKING GOING IN THE NEXT FIVE YEARS?

The beginning of 1985 will see over three million IBM PC/XTs
and compatibles installed and used in corporations, industry,
communications, education, research, government, the military,
and in the home. By the end of 1987 this may well grow to over six
million. Of this number, the majority will be in environments
where there is more than one PC and probably less than ten.
Environments in which data, programs and peripherals will need
to be shared by local area networks (LANs).

In addition, the advent of the IBM PC AT creates a whole
new generation of more expensive computers that will require
networking to reduce costs. That market will certainly be as large,
if not larger, than the current PC market because of the added
power and speed of these machines. The fact that IBM has gone
ahead with this advanced version, the PC AT, signals other companies to follow, starting the cycle all over again.

175

THE IBM STAMP OF APPROVAL

Of equal importance is IBM's coaxial cable local area network, the PC Network, which implements a CSMA/CD bus architecture in a 75-ohm coaxial environment. Thanks to IBM, there will now be a standard local area network environment using this low-cost, readily available, CATV type coaxial 75-ohm cable.

As IBM came into the PC marketplace legitimizing the personal computer, IBM is now impacting the next generation of personal computers and providing a significant credibility boost for the potential LAN market. Prospective users who have been looking for a clear LAN direction now can observe that the 75-ohm, CSMA/CD bus architecture is the standard coaxial environment.

It was two years ago that a group of Silicon Valley entrepreneurs at Orchid Technology in Fremont, California, pioneered the development and sales of the first high-performance, low-cost local area network for the IBM PC and compatibles using a 75-ohm coax bus architecture. The advantages of the 75-ohm CATV coax medium was recognized to offer a low cost connection system with the ability to provide networked systems for either low-cost baseband or higher performance broadband.

THE NETWORK EVOLUTION

Tying together clusters of PCs to enhance productivity and lower costs is a logical decision, but practical only when gains clearly outweigh the overall costs of implementation. There is no "LAN Consumer's Guide" to aid buyers in making this determination or in comparing the very distinct differences in LAN systems available.

Local area networking systems were originally architectured very much like multi-user systems tying users together via dumb terminals connected to a single centralized processor as a means of sharing that processor's resources and data. In networking, the shared resources and data also usually reside on a single processor called a Server. "User" positions are generally personal computers which have both local intelligence and processing capability.

176

WHAT CAN I EXPECT FOR THE FUTURE?

RETAINING PERSONAL PC PERFORMANCE

The user should not have to give up any of his local PC capability. One should be able to enjoy the performance and speed of a single user PC while benefiting from the shared resources, programs and data of a network. It is possible to have the best of both worlds in a "Distributed Network": the capabilities and performance of a single user and the essential capabilities of a Local Area Network.

THE NETWORK OF THE FUTURE "DISTRIBUTED NETWORK"

Rather than load everything—shared programs and data—on a single network Server, these shared resources can be distributed to user positions. One of the first ways to implement a "distributed network" is a system architecture that permits the use of multiple, low-cost, non-dedicated Servers. Multiple Servers not only permit the sharing and distribution of the work load over several Servers, but increase system reliability should a Server go down. This type of Server can not only share its resources with other network users, but it can be used by an operator, thus eliminating the need to tie up expensive dedicated equipment solely for network purposes.

MULTIPLE VOLUME DESIGNATIONS PUBLIC/PRIVATE VOLUMES

A true "distributed" system must be able to permit the division of the shared drive(s) into multiple volumes in order to provide private, as well as shared, disk space. The software must permit these volumes to be individually designated as private (individual) or as public (shared). The latter should further allow the granting of access only to those users who have permission. Such an implementation provides the security and large storage benefits of a single user and the efficient resource and file sharing that only a network can provide.

INCREASING PC SPEED AND
OVERALL PERFORMANCE

Whether at a local user PC, or a network Server, or in a "distributed network," a user should be able to utilize as much memory as needed. He should be able to continue to take advantage of recognized single user capabilities such as RAM disk to provide high-speed access of programs and data stored in RAM that electronically emulates a disk drive.

In addition, a "distributed network" should include other high-speed disk access capabilities that are not generally available. For example, Disk Caching, which is like an automatic RAM Disk, provides high-speed access to programs and data. When implemented properly, Disk Caching automatically retains the most used programs and data while periodically backing up data to the designated disk drive. RAM Disk and Disk Caching not only provide dramatic reductions in disk access time, but faster overall program execution of programs.

PC-TO-PC-TO-NETWORK-TO-NETWORK
COMMUNICATIONS

The inclusion of an immediate interactive PC-to-PC communications capability as well as an optional, sophisticated, true electronic mail system are musts in any LAN and essential especially in a "distributed network." They should permit communications not only within the network, but optionally outside the network to other networks or individual PCs, even over modems to remote locations.

SINGLE BOARDS WITH NETWORKING
AND MULTIFUNCTION

An innovative approach to solving real problems is demonstrated by a combination multifunction and network product called PCnet BLOSSOM(tm). It provides the multifunction features of memory expansion to 384K, a clock/calendar with a unique alarm

178

WHAT CAN I EXPECT FOR THE FUTURE?

feature, a parallel and serial port, and PCnet networking, all using just one card slot. This is the only product of its kind that permits both multifunction and networking capabilities in PCs having only one full-size slot such as the IBM PC Portable.

NETWORKS OF THE FUTURE

The future is going to require that those who want to participate in the LAN market be prepared to offer something new and innovative that provides dramatic increases in productivity at substantially lower costs. Of equal importance is the ease of use, implementation, and sales of a network system, especially in light of the continuing list of enhancements being made available.

INDEX